P

"A father's serial impro[...]
and led to a maze of sel[...]
minute that this is a story illuminated by anything dimmer
than the brightest constellation. I leave these pages so grateful
for this story, for the author's bravery and honesty, and for this
stunning illustration of how writing can carry us through."
SUZANNE STREMPEK SHEA,
AUTHOR OF SONGS FROM A LEAD-LINED ROOM

"The psychological abuse Troisi endured as a child had my fists
clenching in rage. It is almost a relief when she at last finds
escape—in drugs, in codependent love, on the open road. But
this is a story of powerful recovery in the truest sense of the
word, the journey of a woman who reclaims a sense of home in
the sanctity of the self."
DOMENICA RUTA,
NEW YORK TIMES BEST SELLING AUTHOR OF WITH OR WITHOUT YOU

"There's an element of the mythic in Gina Troisi's memoir: the
evil stepmother, the father with misplaced family loyalties,
the daughter whose light eventually shines. Except here the
tale—as with much of real life—is riddled with addiction, both
substance and sexual. And the heroine is far more likely to
wear broken sandals than crystal slippers. Unlike Cinderella,
Troisi's journey to royalty (read sanity and acceptance) isn't
magical; it's slow and hard-won. The story isn't less miraculous
for that, but more so."
SUE WILLIAM SILVERMAN,
AUTHOR OF HOW TO SURVIVE DEATH AND OTHER INCONVENIENCES

"In prose both lucid and visceral, Gina Troisi chronicles her
progress through a very harsh landscape, one marked by casual
cultural horrors and punishing intimate ones, the effects of
conceit, emotional numbness and addiction on the part of
others—a parent, step-parent, lover—that can entangle a
caring person in pointless love and profound confusion. The
narrator is remarkably honest about what she suffered and
learned but also how she kept a thread of herself alive. How she
comes through is inspiring in the basic sense—spirit making
her whole, spirit finding itself in words."
BARON WORMSER,
AUTHOR OF SONGS FROM A VOICE AND THE ROAD WASHES OUT IN SPRING

ABOUT THE AUTHOR

Gina Troisi's work has appeared in numerous literary journals and anthologies, including *Fourth Genre, The Gettysburg Review, Fugue, Under the Sun, Flyway: Journal of Writing & Environment*, and elsewhere. Her stories and essays have been recognized as finalists in several national contests, including the 2020 Iron Horse Literary Review Trifecta Award in Fiction, the 2018 New Letters Publication Award in Fiction, American Literary Review's Creative Nonfiction Contest, 2018, and others. She has taught classes and workshops in both traditional and nontraditional settings, including writing workshops for female adult survivors of sexual assault. She lives in coastal Maine.

Find out more about her at
gina-troisi.com

THE

ANGLE OF

FLICKERING

LIGHT

Gina Troisi

Vine Leaves Press
Melbourne, Vic, Australia

The Angle of Flickering Light
Copyright © 2021 Gina Troisi

All rights reserved.
Print Edition
ISBN: 978-1-925965-48-3
Published by Vine Leaves Press 2021
Melbourne, Victoria, Australia

Cover design by Jessica Bell
Interior design by Amie McCracken

A catalogue record for this book is available from the National Library of Australia

For my mother,
who taught me love

Author's Note

This is a work of memory. I have done my best to recreate
conversations, settings, and events, and to transform
them into a work of art that accurately represents the
emotional landscape of each moment. In many cases,
I have changed names, places, and identifying factors
in order to protect the privacy of others. In some cases,
I have merged, compressed, or omitted details for the
sake of narrative clarity. This story is written from my
perspective alone.

TABLE OF CONTENTS

Part I:
A Hunger

LEFT BEHIND

At five years old, I sat "Indian style" on the foot of my father's bed, alone in his new condo. I'd gathered his ballpoint pens from the desk in the corner, and began assessing the pictures of women adorning the pens; they wore spiked high heels and bright-colored leotards and bikinis, and blue, sequined triangular tops that reminded me of my older sisters' dance recital costumes. Their miniature figures pronounced behind sparkles and strings, their bodies splayed into decorative shapes. I tipped them upside down, and their sparse garments fell off—they were proportioned women, with hardened pink nipples and clumps of dark hair between their legs. I clothed and unclothed them with the flick of my wrist, turned them upside down, then right side up again. They were grown up, like my mother, whom my father had just left. I was mesmerized by these ladies, by their full, buoyant breasts, by the inner curves of thighs that made a hollowed out space for their private parts to breathe. I lay down, watching their clothes fall piece by piece, nestling myself into the cushion of the king-sized bed.

The ladies made me think not only of my mother, but also of the faceless women my father rambled on about while out to eat at our favorite Italian restaurant. My sisters and I sat silent, letting him reiterate that Brenda, his secretary who'd quickly become his girlfriend, had nothing to do with my parents' impending divorce, that he'd been cheating on my mother for years, with all kinds of women, including prostitutes.

"Your mother just didn't want to admit it. She kept her head in the sand. Remember her friend, Marla?" Marla had lived with us for a while when she needed a place to stay in between moves. "I slept with her, too—we had an affair for two years while your mother and I were together. Ask her."

When we arrived home from dinner crying, we gathered in my oldest sister's room. My mother came in to find us sitting on the bed. "What happened?" she asked.

Krista was twelve, so she did most of the talking. "He said he's been cheating on you for years, that you knew. That every time he went on a business trip, it was never for business."

While my mother listened, I kneeled behind Krista, and began to pop the cysts on her back. I worked around the straps of her tank top, performing a job I always volunteered for, since she couldn't reach. My sisters talked fast, repeated my father's words, the gestures he'd made, how he acted as if we must have known about his mistresses all along. I concentrated on squeezing, on trying to find the pointed heads on the bumps of her skin. "Harder," she usually said. "Until all the pus comes out. Until they start bleeding." But today, she didn't tell me what to do, just waited for my mother's response.

"I can't believe he told you those things," my mother said. She looked at the orange walls, the baskets of necklaces made of white seashells and gold nuggets, stacks of *Teen Magazine* and Prince's first albums on cassette tapes. She stood there with a blank look in her eyes, the face of someone who no longer recognized her house, or her daughter's bedroom.

I waited for the yellowish cream, held a tissue to catch a glob when it emerged. Then, the speck of blood. I chimed in: "He said he's been having affairs since the seventies."

My mother seemed shocked, and her lip quivered, as if she didn't know what else to say. She made no indication that my father's statements weren't true. She only said, "He never should have told you any of that."

I liked that I was good at this job, maneuvering these small red mounds, judging when to squeeze harder and when to ease up. I had no worries about scars, since no one would be able to see them, and I felt a kind of satisfaction when the sticky fluid appeared, like the purging of something, but I didn't know what.

I thought of when my father lived here with us, in this brown house on a cul-de-sac, where I built snow igloos and plucked frogs from ponds with the neighborhood kids: his blaring records in the living room, John Denver's "You Fill up my Senses" and Cat Stevens's "Morning Has Broken"; his teaching me how to scramble cheese and black pepper into eggs; his arriving home from a trip to Japan with red, blue, and yellow kimonos for my sisters and me; his taking us to pick out a Christmas tree each year. These memories had suddenly become tweaked and clouded, side-swiped by thoughts of the women he was with on the Japanese vacation with his buddy, who was also cheating on his wife, and a few months back when he and my sister came home from picking out the Christmas tree and she, not understanding that it was a secret, said, "Brenda got the good one," my mom's head jerking toward him, her face hot with anger.

Already, I had grown used to my father's absence. My mother still drove me to kindergarten, *The Little Friend's Learning Center*, in the mornings. When she picked me up in the afternoon, she still wore her jogging clothes and we still sang along to Lionel Richie's "All Night Long" and Laura Branigan's "Gloria" on our way to pick up my sisters from dance lessons. The only time I had counted on seeing my father was before he left for work in the mornings. After he brushed his teeth with baking soda and shaved his face, stuck a piece of tissue on the spot on his chin where he constantly cut himself, he tied his tie, and grabbed his briefcase. I'd stand in the living room crying, and say, "Please don't leave me" over and over. He'd throw me up to the skylight and catch me, then give me a kiss and walk out the door.

*

In the condo, I lathered my five-year-old legs with Nair hair removal cream, and glided my sister's razor up the front of my shins. I knew what women were supposed to look like. I was used to seeing naked ladies, their shapes embellished in the molds of ice cube trays my father kept in the freezer, their silhouettes knitted into his black winter hat to make their own white space, their blank faces and prominent breasts hugging his head.

During the year my father lived at the condo, we arrived to find notes trailing from the front door and into the living room, through the hallway and up the stairs to the bedroom, finally reaching his bed. I sounded out the repetitious lines, "For my lover" and "From your lover," that began and ended each vignette, individual notes taped neatly around pieces of uneaten chocolate. We picked them up but didn't unfold the paper to see the messages inside, and he laughed as we gathered them together, piling them on the desk in his bedroom. We knew then that we would be moved out as Brenda moved in, our roles in his life diminishing, our important jobs of holding wallet, money clip, and keys in our small purses obsolete. She'd be the one going for four-wheel drives in the woods with him; taking trips to the dump with garbage bags covering the windshield while he stuck his head outside the driver's side window to see the road; she'd go sailing with him, and when the boat tipped over, she wouldn't be the one caught underneath the sail gasping for air, terrified that no one would find her to pull her up. We, who had not yet grown into women, would be left behind.

*

Not long after that day in my sister's bedroom, I accompanied my mother on a shopping trip to Loehmann's, her favorite department store. I trailed behind her between racks of clothes, touched the ceramic hands of poised mannequins and followed her into a dressing room lined with mirrors, into a separate stall big enough for the both of us. Now that my father had moved out, she was shopping for clothes to wear to interviews for a job she would hopefully find. She was preparing to return to work after having stayed home for several years.

I sat on the bench in the dressing room, my short legs dangling over the platform while she slipped a blouse over her head, adjusted her shoulder pads, and nodded at her green eyes in the mirror. I smiled at the shade of blue silk, awaited the ice cream she promised to get me after a day of being good, of letting her take her time. My mother's eyes seemed lit up as she checked herself out in the mirror, turning to her left and right, slipping her stockings off and sliding her slender feet into red flats. I realize now her wide eyes were most likely a sign of high alert, anticipation of the upheaval to come, but that day my world consisted only of my mother's bright eyes and the mint chocolate chip ice cream I would eat in a few hours. On some level, I must have known that my father was probably off with his mistress, or possibly late to pick up my sister who sat at dancing school alone, all of the other kids gone, wondering if he'd ever show, but this was beyond my peripheral vision. Within my lens, in this radiant dressing room with my mother's smooth skin and potential new outfit, everything still seemed possible.

*

When my mother needed a break from tending to three young children, which was often, she dropped me off at my grandparents' (my father's parents') house. It was a heart-colored house in a quaint green neighborhood in Massachusetts—a ranch house with white shutters and perfectly manicured hedges that lined the neat, square patch of lawn. I played waitress there using clear glass ashtrays, some of which I left empty, while filling others with egg-shaped gelatin candies. They were sugar covered, as if sprinkled with shards of crystals. I placed them on coffee tables, in front of imaginary people sitting on the loveseat, and on end tables. I created stacks of clutter, stashing the small dishes in corners of the house like jewels.

My grandfather, Nanu, received the empty ashtrays with delight. "Thank you, GG! This is delicious," he said, opening his mouth wide to accept invisible salads and chicken soup, scooping them up with imaginary forks and spoons.

My Nana, Regina, sat with crossed legs, holding a cigarette between her first and second fingers, the paper around them staining her flesh yellow. I envied her ritual, fixated on the red, glowing ember, smoke rising from the smoldering paper in her upturned hand, and I fantasized about taking a puff or two. It was around this time, when I was seven or eight, that my father taught my sisters and me how to smoke. The three of us surrounded him in the house of a family friend while he, whom I'd never known to smoke, lit a cigarette and passed it around so we each got a turn, coached us on how to inhale and exhale. My sisters coughed and complained of the taste and smell, but the paper felt at home between my small fingers. I crossed my legs, let them dangle over the chair, breathed in and out with skill.

Nana offered me patchwork ice cream topped with vanilla cookies, which I eagerly accepted. Together, we watched black-and-white murder mysteries on television, and I fell in love with Perry Mason. She'd let me sit in Nanu's recliner, and I'd tuck myself into the large seat wearing her rosaries around my neck. The onyx beads busied me for hours, as I recited Hail Marys and Our Fathers. When Nanu finished painting on canvases in the basement, he'd come upstairs to listen to me sounding the prayers, and smile. "Did your grandmother teach you that?" When I was done, he'd tickle me until I fell out of the chair—until I was exhausted from laughter.

My Nanu glanced in his wife's direction with love, his mouth curved in a half-joking grin. "What do you think, Reggie?" He'd playfully poke her in the ribs while stirring homemade tomato sauce, and fling a dishtowel over his shoulder. It would land clumsily across his neck, and she'd smile. He hugged her for what seemed like minutes.

At bedtime, I molded myself into my grandparents' bed wearing Nanu's worn yellow t-shirts that hung just below my knees. He'd pinch my cheek while I said my prayers and say, "Ciao Bella." When I was done, I'd curl up next to him with my head on his strong shoulder, and fall into a deep sleep.

UNTIL THE
MORNING COMES

I dreaded the overnight with my father and Brenda.
I stared out the backseat window at the northern
New Hampshire mountains, my duffel bag at my feet,
as I was dragged along to a parents' weekend hosted
by my stepsister Jocelyn's summer camp. The pine
trees were dense with green, the mountains blazed
with hints of red sun.

My father drove with a closed-mouth smile, occasionally talking to Brenda as if they were alone on
their honeymoon. "Isn't this pretty, honey?"

She caressed his neck while he looked ahead at
the road, his hand on her thigh. "It is. I love you,
Joe," she said. Her brown hair was highlighted with
blonde, her profile prominent, her large nose pointed
toward him.

"I love you too, honey." His smile was like that of
a school boy who had his first crush. Last time the
three of us were in the car together, Billy Joel's "She's
Always a Woman" came on the radio, and my father
said, "This song always reminds me of Brenda,"
speaking about her in third person even though
she was right there. Other times he said, "Brenda's
posture is one of the first things that attracted me to
her," and she leaned back further, her small breasts

poking out while he waited for a response I never gave. What most people considered to be private, they spoke of out in the open. Even though I was used to this, I couldn't help but think back to when my parents were still married, an image of Brenda straddling my father on his office desk tearing through my mind.

*

The year my parents separated, Brenda officially graduated from my father's secretary to his wife. That year, before the separation, my mother made a surprise visit to Brenda's apartment complex on a weekday at lunchtime, and my father's car was parked in the lot. When my mother knocked, Brenda answered the door in her white terry cloth bathrobe while my father emerged from the bedroom.

Brenda said, "It's not what it looks like."

*

We passed through a small town filled with antique shops, hardware stores, and a small grocer, as we neared the bed-and-breakfast in Jackson, where we'd sleep before heading to the camp in the morning. Brenda said, "Gina, did I tell you Jocelyn's playing tennis? *And* losing weight?" She didn't turn around but looked at me in the side view mirror, waiting for my response.

I nodded. "Yup, you said that. That's great." She expected me to smile, so I did.

She always talked about Jocelyn this way, anticipating praise, as if taking credit for her daughter's giftedness, her athleticism, her creativity, but to her face she called her a bitch, a drama queen, spoiled and rotten. Brenda was the type of woman who insisted that I visit my father's house, but once I arrived, she announced that she'd bought two tickets for a Boston Celtics game, or a play, and they'd leave me there alone for the night. She was the type of woman who said I was too skinny only a year after refusing me snacks because I was too fat. She was the type of woman who said, "Let's go school shopping," but once we got to the department store, she insisted on taking a detour to the lingerie department to pick out something to wear with my father. She was a woman who, no matter how erratic or irrational her mood, was easier to please than to argue with.

I knew that Jocelyn's camp was for rich kids, and even though my father was footing the bill for it, I didn't live the same life as Jocelyn. I lived most of the time with my mother. We ate leftovers and clipped coupons, made purchases according to what was on sale, never turned the heat above sixty degrees. My mother worked odd, erratic jobs—evenings at a tractor trailer company, days as a travel agent booking trips for other people, sporadic hours hustling through parking lots passing out fliers for the herbs and vitamins she sold.

At twelve, the youngest of my father's daughters, I had not yet begun to run wild, but I was thinking about it. I was on the cusp of girlhood and woman-hood, the age where everything that had already happened was surfacing, impressions either fading or sticking. A few years before, I called my mother to tell her that Brenda refused to let me eat between meals because I was too fat, and when I hung up, my father told me that he had been listening on the line, that I wouldn't be allowed to make or receive phone calls from my mother any longer. Now, each time I thought of my hunger, I thought harder about the bulges of flesh near my armpits, or the way my inner thighs rubbed together. I was obsessed with my thinness. I jogged through my mother's neighborhood for miles, listening to loud music, Bon Jovi and Madonna, spent hours on the living room carpet doing Jane Fonda's workouts, stood naked in front of the mirror assessing pouches of skin, devising plans to get rid of it. It would not be long before I'd be throwing up an apple even if it was the only thing I ate that day. Not long before I'd refuse to let anything sit inside me long enough to be absorbed, before emptiness became so familiar that I began to crave it.

I was looking forward to seeing Jocelyn. Since my sisters were old enough to be absent from the weekend visits at my father's house, Jocelyn and I had been stuck together for the past few years, subjected to Brenda's erratic rules—one day we were punished for eating at the kitchen table, and another day reprimanded for taking food anywhere else. We listened to her spew demands and we prepared for her backlash; we must be up and showered by a specific hour, eat certain foods at precise times, appear in certain rooms when she deemed appropriate, vanish when she saw fit, and always wear our happiest faces. Brenda saved her most unnerving conduct for when she and I were alone together, like when she drove me to a house in their town to show me where a woman was brutally beaten and murdered by her husband. Naturally, I was relieved by Jocelyn's presence.

*

When our parents first moved in together, Jocelyn and I were seven and six. We played with Barbies and argued about who got to use which ones; I couldn't relate to her demand for attention, or the way she'd suddenly isolate herself, burying her face in a book. "She could read at four years old," Brenda always said. I hated Jocelyn's flimsy paper dolls and the unicorns decorating her room. I hated the waterbed I had to sleep in with her, how I was the invisible visitor crammed into her bed—hated how, for years, we'd receive the same birthday and Christmas presents in different colors, as if we were the same person, especially when we couldn't have been more different. Over time though, I'd become thankful for Jocelyn's presence, our relationship like cellmates who got along most of the time because we understood the small spaces we maneuvered, the precepts we adhered to in order to survive. One thing Jocelyn and I began to have in common was our desire to run away. We'd pack trash bags filled with clothes and wander out into the neighborhood, circling the block, looking for anywhere else to go.

*

When we arrived in Jackson, Jean welcomed us into her bed-and-breakfast, greeting us with pamphlets of the area, mentioning waterfalls to visit, hikes to take, parks to picnic at. I loathed these houses—the long winding Victorian staircases, the pink floral prints on the blankets, the canopies over the beds, the shared bathrooms with old-fashioned bathtubs, the kind with feet. What should have been beautiful was not; the grand mantles and the antique paintings were overrun by thoughts of ghosts waiting in the stairwell, people locked up in attics, children trapped in secret passages where no one found them.

Mostly, it was our act I despised, the one where Brenda nudged me with jokes while in front of others, as if we were mother and daughter, or worse, friends. She'd occasionally do this at home too, telling me how my father was good in bed at the dinner table, or asking if she could braid my hair. Later, she'd retract her friendship, tell me that I was nothing but my mother's clone, her evil mimic.

Jean helped us with our bags, delivered us to a room. It had a queen-sized bed with nightstands on both sides, and a daybed against the opposite wall. She nodded at me and pointed to the daybed. "And this bed is for you—this room is perfect for three." I had always secretly wanted one of these beds, the kind Candace Cameron had on the television show *Full House*, the kind of bed that transformed into a couch, turning a bedroom into a living room. I studied the comforter, its rose print like something out of a cheesy romance novel, and I contemplated how I'd change the spread if it were mine, sew something myself, like a patchwork quilt of different-sized stars.

*

That night, I sat on the bed with my legs crossed, my duffel bag placed neatly on its edge, and unpacked my hair ties and pajamas. My father had left the room, and Brenda started opening the tall cabinet doors and rummaging around, looking past hangers and an iron and the Bible. I wanted to ask what she was doing, but I didn't talk to her unless I had to. I was used to her withholding information when I wanted it, and providing it when I didn't, like when she told me about a woman who went to a fortune teller, but the psychic said her future was unreadable—later that day, the woman got hit by a car and died. Brenda left the room and I let out a sigh.

When she came back, she was wheeling a folded-up army cot. She wore an expressionless smile, the kind of smile meant to hide what she was really thinking. She opened the door to a closet wide enough to hang clothes, but narrow. She wheeled the cot into the closet and started to unfold it, but the space was too cramped to unbend it all the way; the walls touched every inch of its metal rods. She stood outside of the closet, struggling to stretch the cot out completely, but the crease in the middle made a V shape, a bend where a person's waist should be.

My father walked into the room from who knows where, and I expected him to be curious, but he began putting his pants and t-shirts into drawers.

"What are you doing? What is that for?" I finally asked.

"It's for you," she said, with her stiff smile.

All three of us had nodded when Jean pointed to the daybed, and said, "And this bed is for you—this room is perfect for three." For a moment I wondered if I'd dreamt that exchange, but then I remembered who Brenda was. *It's not what it looks like.*

The cot was bare except for a thin white sheet bunched in the middle. I studied the cot as if sizing myself for a coffin. I doubted that my five-foot body would even fit into that closet. Brenda turned around and looked at me, her smile turned to ice, her beady eyes staring right through me. I could never tell what she was really looking at—her stare empty, unreadable.

I half believed my father might think that Brenda's idea was odd since the daybed was obviously intended for me, but he was unfazed. He told Brenda, "I just met this great couple, Jen and Steve, downstairs. Their daughter goes to the camp too." My father always referred to Jocelyn as his daughter. By this time, my grandparents had moved from Massachusetts to Florida, but recently, when they were home for a visit, my father demanded that my Nanu, who painted portraits of my sisters and me, paint one from Jocelyn's school picture as well. "She's your granddaughter." My father raised his voice in an adjacent room while my grandmother rocked in her chair nervously, and slipped me a twenty.

"Don't tell anyone," she said, attempting to make up for my father's words, for the way he always said the wrong thing in the wrong way, for how he never had any recollection or remorse.

My father continued: "I was telling them how it's our daughter's first summer there—about how much she loves it. I mentioned The Harrison School, and they seemed pretty interested." The Harrison School was a boarding school they wanted Jocelyn to apply to.

Brenda said, "That's great, Joe," and spread a wool blanket on the cot even though it was seventy-five degrees in the room. "Here you go, Gina," she said without looking at me.

I looked at the clock: eight-thirty. *What am I going to do in there?* I had my journal and my book, *Heaven*, by V.C. Andrews. I didn't even bother to look at my father, who, since he'd married Brenda, seemed to possess no thoughts of his own.

I was not even close to tired, but I climbed up onto the cot, leaving my pajamas on the edge of the daybed. The cot crooked my lower back, my legs still, my body beginning to cramp. I wanted to stretch my limbs, wanted to dissolve into the sheets, sink down into the crevice, break through the floor and slide down some magical chute until I hit the ground and broke free from this place. "I wanted to read," I said, half hoping she or *they* would change their minds. "There's no light in here."

I heard shuffling, and then Brenda shoved a lamp, the kind that stood on the floor, into the closet, but there was no outlet, so she closed the door on the cord. "Problem solved."

This was not a room. This wasn't even one fiftieth of a room—it was the length of my body. I thought about Jean, the owner of the house, how she'd probably be alarmed to know that the daybed was empty. *See, she'd said. Here is your bed. Perfect for three people.* She was the kind of woman who probably tapped maple trees and kept bees—the type of woman who fed her children farm-fresh eggs from free-range chickens she raised herself. She was the kind of woman who was a nurturer, a caregiver. Brenda, on the other hand, was the type of woman who stole kids' fathers, sent them away to summer camps and boarding schools, shoved them into the closet. She was the type of woman who kept *The Joy of Sex* on the nightstand and left the bedroom door open for everyone to see. She was the kind of woman who determined your fate.

I assumed the reason they wanted me in the closet was so they could have sex, and I was sure they did, although I never heard it. I was thankful for the air conditioner's loud hum, relieved that the bed was absent of mirrors on the inside of the canopy, unlike their bed at home. In the closet, I realized how skilled I'd become at blocking out what was going on around me, how I was able to sink so deep into myself that even I was left wondering where I'd gone. In the closet, I remembered a line from the movie *Mommie Dearest*, a movie Brenda had turned on time and time again: "If she doesn't like you, she can make you disappear."

In the morning, at breakfast, having barely slept, I nibbled at the fruit salad on the table while watching guests down greasy sausage links and pancakes with syrup. My father and Brenda engaged in the small talk that happens in someone's home rented out to visitors; they talked about the general store down the road, the view of the lake, how the hiking trails were mobbed this time of year, while I was silent. They asked people where they were from, where they were headed, introduced me as their daughter. I mostly looked down at my plate. I avoided the eyes of strangers, afraid they'd see through me—that their eyes would swallow me if they found out the truth— that I was perpetually held captive by these two, that I could not trust them, that I had nowhere else to go.

*

We drove toward the camp down a long dirt drive. Yards in front of us, cabins were tucked into a large hill, and we moved closer to a village of tiny wooden houses. To the left were tennis courts and to the right an outdoor theater. We'd watch the girls play tennis in white uniforms, row crew, stage performances. The camp was designed to encourage their independence and character, to help them feel proud of their accomplishments and develop their own ideas and opinions. Even though the camp was for girls ranging from nine to fifteen—even though I fell in the middle of this age bracket, I couldn't imagine being up on a stage, changing into fitted uniforms when my own clothes were sizes too big—I didn't want people looking at or listening to me.

Brenda turned to me. "Did you know Jocelyn has a beautiful singing voice?"

The camp activities seemed trivial to me, and I wasn't interested in sports. Soon, I'd be the child failing gym class because I refused to change my clothes on the rare days when I didn't refuse to go to school. I'd be the one looking for escape, taking acid at friends' beach houses and running along the strip being chased by police. I'd spend my summers in friends' crowded cars clouded with smoke, passing wine bottles, crushing up pills; my idea of after school like those specials they played on television, the ones where the kids snort meth in the high school bathrooms instead of going to softball practice. I would not be Jocelyn with her summer camp and her boarding school and her expensive bras, her option of applying to any university, and I knew this at age twelve. I knew the kind of life that I was drawn to, the kind of life that I was on the verge of making.

*

Even though it was small, I loved the cabin Jocelyn was living in, the way her roommate's bed was only a foot away, the way their books were stacked on the small window sills, the handmade shelves. I loved the trunk at the end of the bed—the concept of packing up our belongings and cramming them into a six-by-four foot space, their presence reinforcing the readiness for adventure. I loved the collages on the walls made in art class, the paintings—I felt alive in the cabin. I wanted to live there, inside the wooded sanctuary with a community of people, listening to the patter of rain, the crunching of leaves.

Next summer, the cabin would become unsafe. Brenda would snoop through all of the letters I'd sent to Jocelyn, make copies of them, and mail them to my mother. She'd call my mother on the phone and recite lines about finishing liquor bottles and smoking pot in my bedroom with the windows wide open, about lying down with boys and another girl, half naked while we let the boys touch us all over. Brenda followed up the phone call with her own letters addressed to my mother—letters blaming my mother for my father's cheating, stating that it was actually her fault, since she "knew all along," but chose to "turn a blind eye." She'd write letters in which she'd call my mother a "bitch," and then draw smiley faces in the space where she signed her name.

*

At dusk, the counselors led us to Campfire Rock, a wooded spot with a clearing overlooking the lake. The sky was purplish black, and the girls wore white dresses that flashed against the darkness. The girls began to sing, some sounding higher while others remained low, each voice adding her own version of a pitch that rose and fell, her own surrender to a changeless, shapeless tone. Although I'd never heard any of these songs, there was one in particular, "Four-Leaf Clover," that, when the girls sang, struck me with an unmistakable ease, a relief I hadn't known I needed until that moment.

There was something about their voices reverberating against one another, the shine of the lake in the background, the burning smell of the campfire being lit in the woods that, when coinciding, carried an unerringness, delivered a moment in time when everything, despite all the imperfections that came before and after it, was exactly as it should be. Surrounded by the faces of proud parents, good parents, I recognized an innocence in the girls' voices, a purity I wanted to consume but knew that I could not. Despite this knowing, when the singing voices ripped through me, I sensed how it might feel to belong, to mesh into this picture like the red and striped maples branching out over the water.

It began to rain, and I slipped my feet out of my sandals and let my toes get soaked, sink into the mud. I hadn't spent much time in the woods other than at parties with bonfires and kegs of beer bought by my older sisters and the older siblings of friends, and I was drawn to the birches, to the lake, the dirt. I wanted to sleep on the earth and be swallowed by the wide-open space. There, in the woods, listening to the sound of the girls' voices in unison, the wind rattling the trees and swallows sailing above the lake, the dying sun glimmering on the water, I knew that the world was larger than my father and Brenda, and I felt a restlessness, a hunger that could not contain itself.

WILD AGAINST
A SEA OF GREEN

"The trees are alive, the trees are alive." I said this over and over. David, my best friend since the third grade, and I were drinking mushroom tea, riding around our southern New Hampshire hometown in the back of another friend's convertible. The top was down, and she yelled at me every time I stood up in the back seat. It was May, the time of year when you could almost see the trees become a deeper green with each moment, New England natives wild with nervous energy that had been building the entire winter; I wanted to get a good view. It was beginning to rain, and the wind was picking up, branches waving, spraying drops that wet my face like holy water. This wind reminded me of flying down the road on the back of my uncle's Harley, our minimal conversation when we stopped at a red light. It was the same quick conversation we'd had each time he called.

"You been behavin'?" he asked.

"Yup."

"That's no fun." He laughed and shook his head before the light turned green and we sailed off down the road.

The wind was a reminder of his arrest the following

week or month after he said this—they found cocaine underneath the visor of his car, or heroin stashed underneath the seat of his motorcycle. When Uncle Dicky called from jail, my Nanu would leave the golf course, or my father would abruptly abandon work or home or a family vacation to go bail him out, to "talk some sense" into him. Uncle Dicky would go back to rehab, stay clean for a while, then do it all over again. The wind was a reminder of a line in the poem his cousin read at his funeral: *In the wind I believe, he somehow felt free.*

It rustled my hair. I shut and opened my eyes, squinted and blinked, spats of sun beating on our skin, grayish storm clouds patching up pieces of sky.

"Gina, sit down," my friend, the driver, said again. "Put on your seatbelt."

"If I'm destined to die, a seatbelt won't do anything." She was annoyed, but I meant what I said. I didn't want to die, but I did believe in destiny.

David passed me a bottle of Jack, but I shook my head. We had made mushroom tea, and that was so much better than booze. The trees were colossal guardians walking past one another. Birches, white pines, red maples. Dogwoods, beeches, green ash. In the car, we were part of a doll's village, a miniature playland. We weaved in between the trees, curved around them as if through a forest on our way to a castle.

What road are we on? Winding, venturing, unpredictable. We drove by the town dump, past the post office, the drug store, chain restaurants, through intersections and traffic lights. We'd grown up in this New Hampshire town on the border of

Massachusetts, where we did a lot of driving along both busy and rural roads. We drove for hours, sometimes for days, not knowing where we were going or why, only knowing that we needed to.

That day, we headed to a closed children's camp, where we explored empty cabins. The miniature houses were tucked into a forest of maples and shagbarks that blocked the view of the nearby lake. We sat in an isolated cabin on the outskirts of the campground, the echo of our voices drawing me in and out, the sounds of syllables consuming me. The sky crackled, the *booms* of thunder reverberated inside the tiny wooden structure nestled in between the trees. I was usually drawn to the water, but today I wanted to sit on the steps of the abandoned cabin, sheltered by the edge of its A-frame roof, smoke a cigarette, and think about the way I'd splash its inside with paint if I lived here.

David gave me a massage while we passed a pipe back and forth, joked about the last time we hung out in the woods while tripping, running from the police and their K-9s. We had lost one another, and when I reached the end of the woods alone, I found myself on a familiar road in our town. A moment later, a kid we went to school with slowed down, opened the door, and let me jump in. "Need a ride, Gina?" We could not get over the coincidence.

"Meant to be," David said. Bolts of lightning. Jagged lines down, then across the sky. The rain the sound of a waterfall; it skirted off the roof, missing us. We heard breaks and pops as twigs and branches split. This rain carried the smell of summer with it, wood chips and mulch.

When it slowed down, we put up our hoods and walked far down the main road, until we reached a dirt path that led to a fort we built in junior high. We stumbled around the forest searching for scraps of dry firewood while the rain dissipated. We arranged the wood in the shape of a teepee and built a fire, smoked cigarettes and pot as we warmed up, the hours of the day slipping away.

*

In school, my classmates were meeting with guidance counselors and applying to colleges. I was not thinking about the future. High school had become a place to drop acid, do bumps of coke and meth in the bathroom, whichever was easiest to get. Stretches of white walls and fluorescent lights. Yellow hallways with no windows, identical doors. Rows of lockers with forgotten combinations. Circles and semi-circles of chairs with desks attached, encompassing and enclosing bodies. Chalkboards with formulas I couldn't read. School had become a place to skip out on, to sign my own hall passes, to forge notes from my mother. My older sister had permission to dismiss me, so I called her from the payphone outside the cafeteria when the acid began to kick in or when I needed to smoke a bowl to relieve my hangover. When she wasn't around, I snuck out into the woods during study hall, or just walked out the front doors, down the hill to my car.

*

The next month, in June, a friend and I took a ride to Hampton Beach, a half hour north of our hometown.

His father had just died after a long battle with cancer, his brother was unable to speak from grief, and he needed a break from the quiet of his family's house. The sand shone alongside a cement strip littered with garbage, sidewalks filled with loitering teens in and out of arcades and cottages. We often went to house parties that got busted, and when the cops came, we ran down to the ocean in bare feet, trying not to step on broken glass and dirty condoms. My friend and I remembered that people we knew had rented the upstairs of a beach house on S Street, so this became our destination.

We arrived at the house and planted ourselves in the living room with its wood-paneled walls and striped paper, beaded orange lamps, green shag rug. He had some coke for us to share, so we waited for people to scatter. When everyone was gone, we listened to Blind Melon, and he broke the coke into lines, then neat semi-circles dusting the coffee table. When he handed me the dollar bill, I took it from him, told him I was sorry. "I have no idea what it's like to lose someone like that, to watch them suffer. I can't even pretend to know." The only death I had experienced was my uncle Dicky's, my father's brother who died at thirty-nine, and although his sickness didn't involve medication and experimental treatments, it was inevitable.

"Were you close?" I asked.

"Yeah," he said, snorting the powder, leaning his head back, and letting it drip down his throat, swallowing its numbness.

I thought of my own father, but I didn't say anything about it. I felt guilty because he had lost his. When I thought of my father, I heard his voice slice me open, telling me I was a "spoiled little fucking bitch." One of the last times I saw him was in ninth grade, after he found out I received a D in Phys. Ed. because I refused to change in front of the other girls in the locker room. He drove me to a grocery store parking lot, the smell of leather seats turning my stomach, his voice echoing through the parked car as he hollered: "Why would you be such an asshole?" I was reminded of the therapist he sent me to when I was seven because I was overweight, the other therapist he sent me to when I was twelve and starving myself.

When I thought of him, I told myself: *I am still young. There will be time. We will make amends before one of us dies.* But the truth was that I had been waiting years to be free of him, to run wild, far beyond the mold he created for me, to eradicate my intense self-hatred, the emptiness I felt—to fill myself up with anything, anyone I could get my hands on.

My friend told me it was about forgiveness, about realizing that it wasn't your fault you were abandoned. "At least we got to say goodbye. I bet sudden death is totally different," he said. "People must always think of the last conversation, replaying it in their mind. If you had a fight or something right before. When someone has been sick for a while, it probably doesn't fuck with you as much."

I wondered what their last conversation was, but I didn't ask. "At least he isn't suffering anymore," I offered, my voice speeding up, concentrating on his mouth, his half-spiked, tousled dirty blond hair.

"You're right," he said, his pale skin lined with days of waiting. We decided to forget that people other than us were staying at the cottage; we blew lines off the coffee table for hours. After too much talk of death, and too many sad Blind Melon lyrics, he pulled me from the chair onto the couch, draped me over him like a blanket, kissed me, our hands searching one another's skin like new territory: creases and ridges and ribs. What were we looking for? More.

I hadn't thought of him like this. We were party friends, people who killed time together when they had nothing else to do, but this night was different. I didn't know if it was the intimacy of the first days of summer, the heat, the coke, the sweat, or if we had realized we would be unable to touch one another once we were dead. Lips and tongues, clavicles and earlobes. Hands and arms and stomachs. A leg or an arm knocked over the vase of fake plastic flowers on the end table—the ceramic crashed to the floor, but we didn't stop. The cottage smelled of cheap coffee and even cheaper beer, and his hand was down my pants, underneath the men's boxer briefs I wore as underwear, inside of me.

The screen of the back door creaked. We dipped out of the living room and into an empty bedroom where he climbed on top of me. The coke was gone, but we had more to do, and the sun was rising outside the window. He unzipped my sweatshirt, my pants, touched me everywhere, and I waited for more. He had been going to school to be a mechanic, and he had those hands that looked filthy, but weren't, especially underneath his fingernails where there was a permanent stain. I couldn't see them in this dark bedroom, but I had noticed them before—strong, hardworking blue-collar hands—at this moment, my body their only map.

*

When the door to the bedroom opened, we were half naked. "Sorry," someone said, after stumbling into the bedroom. We realized it was her room, so we put our clothes on, and walked down the street to the water. We sat on the beach and smoked cigarettes, dug our bare feet into the sand, and shielded our eyes from the emerging light while catching glimpses of pink and red, of burning sun. I lay down and made an imprint of my body in the sand, sifted it between my fingers, let it scrape the small of my back, the back of my neck, let it settle into my hair, and closed my eyes.

*

When I found the drug, ecstasy, the only way I was able to describe the feeling it gave me was like this: it was like standing on top of the world. It cleared my memory of the girl I used to be—who was perpetually hungry, who felt a throbbing pulse in her neck, veins constricting as she tiptoed through rooms, almost paralyzed by fear. It wasn't that I preferred it to acid or mushrooms, or even coke, but I found a truth in this pill, an answer I'd been teetering on the edge of, like a piece of gospel a lover whispers while you orgasm, a sensation you can never quite capture in the same way again. The day after, despite my clenched teeth, the sore muscles of my skull, my jaw aching, I'd feel the remnants of euphoria. There was not only a letting go of inhibitions, but an immersion of the senses I was after—the way the expected and mundane suddenly became compelling, even thrilling, like plunging into water and submerging your head for the first time as a small child.

Despite the damage I was doing to my body, there was an idealism that existed inside my core, an optimism that synchronized with the way I wanted to live—free and unconfined, beyond the rules and regulations that had been created for me, the constant limitations and criticism. I wasn't sure if there was any legitimacy to the rumor we heard, that heroin was one of the ingredients in this drug, but I liked the idea of it, not because I wanted to be a junkie, but because I had long understood the desire to slink outside of myself and into an indescribable stillness. I empathized with the desire for the type of serenity addicts described reaching just after they shot up. I understood the chase, and why people got hooked.

When I was on ecstasy, I believed it was impossible for there to be anything more to life than *now*.

*

Another guy, also a friend. We were fooling around in an empty bedroom while someone's mom was out of town. I had opened a capsule of Molly (short for MDMA, the main ingredient in ecstasy), and poured the powder onto a TV dinner tray to snort it—in the process, I spilled a bit onto the rug, and now I was trying to find it.

"Come on, G. Forget about it," he said, and started to unzip my pants. He had been making me laugh, cracking jokes about cars we used to drive in when we were younger, how we made cassette tape mixes of banned heavy metal songs. How he and his friends made a mummy and put it in the middle of the road, so people would run over it and think they hit a person. Someone in the living room of the house was barking like a dog, someone else laughing, and the base of my neck was getting limper, my cheeks warm, my face loosening. We heard bottles smash in the front yard, heard someone else yelling to "Cut it out," but he kept going, started to go down on me. I was trying to focus, but my eyes were still on the rug, looking for glints of lost powder. I saw a tiny yellow flare blending into the beige carpet.

Lying face up on the bed, I reached my arm toward the TV dinner tray next to me, fumbling for the rolled-up dollar bill.

"Wait," I said.

"What are you doing?" he asked.

"Sorry." He stopped, kneeled on the bed, holding the tops of my thighs. "Give me a second. One second," I said. I didn't want to lose it again. He let go, and I hopped off the bed, my bare knees pressed into the rug, grazed the end of the tiny tube against the carpet, and sucked back the bit of powder I'd found. It stung the skin inside my nose, and the bitter taste coated my throat, but I was pleased. He followed me to the floor.

We stayed down on the floor, and he made me moan, but I was becoming free from my body. On the ceiling, cracks were moving, Courtney Love was posing in a short skirt, her pouty pigmented lips capturing me. He was hard up against me, started to press himself into me, but I didn't care. I was swimming around in the poster, drowning in The Doors music playing: "The Crystal Ship." Jim Morrison singing about crying, about flying. I felt his skin against mine, his hand unhooking my bra. He was about to go in, as we kissed. "Shit," he said.

I took a breath. "What?"

He hesitated. "I don't have a condom."

I was afraid of few things, but getting pregnant was one of them. My mother had taken me aside multiple times, pulled me into the bathroom off her bedroom, in front of the vanity mirror. She said, "I've raised three girls. Neither of your sisters has gotten pregnant. Please don't let it be you." Her face was shaded with worry, her lips pursed, both of our reflections staring back at me.

"Okay," I said. My mother didn't put pressure on me to be perfect like the mothers of most girls my age. She didn't try to live through me, to persuade me to have a career I didn't want, or the wedding or marriage she never had. I felt a loyalty to her, but it was not only her voice that stopped me. It was the thought of something foreign attached to me, growing inside of me; it was the thought of something that needed and wanted, that asked for too much. A tiny person to whom I'd never have the capacity to give.

"I'll go to the store," he said. He wanted this badly.

"Okay."

While he was gone, I sat in the living room, beginning to rush, my jaw clenched, my head moving to the music of CDs in the three-disc changer: Janis Joplin and The Doors and The Dead. The house had emptied out. People had left for another party. The girl who lived there was curled up on the couch drinking Boone's Farm wine, and she shared some with me. It tasted of cherries, and it rolled across my tongue and slid down my throat. I told her how much I loved the curtains, the intricate design of embroidered pansies. I told her how pretty she was.

She said she would love to get a car with a diesel engine that ran on vegetable oil, that she wanted to live somewhere warm, somewhere far from New England, where she had an outdoor solar-powered shower.

I agreed that these were magnificent ideas. "I want to learn how to grow herbs," I told her. "To have a garden with lavender and thyme. I don't even need a house, just a tent."

I was not sure what this girl was on, but we went on to discuss how lonely it had been for her as an only child, how her mother, a psychiatrist, never missed a beat. On her daughter, she smelled one drag taken from a cigarette, saw the trace of a hickey, found the shake from a bag of weed at the bottom of the garbage can. "It's brutal," the girl said. I looked around, glad for her that no damage was evident inside the house.

"What is your favorite license plate?" I asked her.

She described the fir tree on the Oregon plate, and the motto of Missouri as the "Show-Me" state. *"What does it mean?"* we asked one another.

She got up to grab some food from the fridge, came back with a block of cheddar and a butter knife. "Want some?" I shook my head; there was no way I could eat real food, but I remembered that I had a Tootsie Pop in my bag, that it might help to relieve the tightness of my jaw. "Is this your journal? I love that," she said, pointing to the bumper sticker stuck to the front of the book, the one with a rose with thorns that resembled hemp plants. On the sticker, italicized words said, *What if a rose was a felony?* Her compliment reminded me of a dream I had been wanting to write down, one that began in a basement filled with pot plants.

When my friend returned, I realized that he had

been gone for a while. "I got pulled over," he said. "They gave me a sobriety test."

"Oh no," I said, looking up from my journal. He was bringing my buzz down. I didn't want to talk about cops.

"Luckily, I passed." He looked at me, raised his chin back toward the bedroom where he went down on me. "Still want to hang out?" he asked.

I looked out the window, saw the yard full of dandelions. Yellow dahlias were blooming in a neighbor's garden. It must have been seventy degrees out. The tangerine lollipop was melting in my mouth, turning to juice and quenching my thirst.

"Maybe another time," I said. I wanted to go outside. There would be another empty house, another car, another guy, but I did not want to waste this high.

He looked at me, confused, taking in the scene of the living room, the girl and me sitting across from one another, the cut-up cheese on the carpet, the sun shining in through the windows. I got up, squeezed his hand, and kissed him on the lips on my way out the front door and into the yard, my feet floating across the grass. I kept moving, my eyes wide as I continued down the road, searching for a nearby trail in the woods.

I did not yet know that this would be the beginning of a path not easily abandoned—that I'd perch myself along the periphery of danger again and again, engage in relationships with men who shared similar fates, dip down into treacherous waters—not knowing whether I'd be able to pull myself out. But today, I sensed only beauty among the chaos, a chaos that seemed to recreate me, to deliver me back to where I came from, and I weaved onto a dirt path, mesmerized by the branches stroking the sky, the rustling of leaves and fluttering of birds, the flashes of red and yellow flowers, wild against a sea of green.

WRAPPED UP IN SKIN, HIDDEN BEHIND EYES

When I was in the third grade, during a weekend visit to my father's house, Brenda picked out a movie for the two of us to watch: *Fatal Attraction*. Sitting on the sectional couch with her feet propped up on the coffee table, Brenda said, "Makes you think twice about where to put your dick." In the film, Dan Gallagher, the lawyer, slept with Alex Forrest when his wife was out of town; he intended for the affair to be a one-night stand, but she began to stalk him and his family. Near the end of the movie, she broke into his house, snuck into the bathroom, and as Dan's wife wiped steam from the mirror, Alex's face was revealed. The mistress was standing behind the wife: her blonde, frosted hair coiled around her face, her mouth solemn and silent. She wore a long white dress with no bra, her nipples shading its sheer fabric, a butcher knife in her hand.

When the movie was over, Brenda looked at me, waited for my response. "Well?" she asked. I said nothing. I nodded the way I always did when Brenda talked about dicks or sex, the way I did when she told me about haunted houses where blood dripped out of the faucets, or kidnappers driving white vans through town. Brenda wore her closed-mouth smile while she gazed at me, then straight ahead, satisfied with my compliance.

*

My father, the lawyer, met women on planes. When I was in college, I called his office and the receptionist giggled, "Oh, hi, Gina. He got tied up." Somewhere over the Atlantic. Somewhere over the Gulf. "He'll be back a couple of days later than expected."

He was a natural when it came to affairs—he moved easily into their illusory territory, into the arms of foreign women. He was the type of man who fell into the life of a woman and allowed her to reshape him, design him as she saw fit. Each woman was his prospect, then his project, then his proprietor.

*

When Brenda was promoted from my father's secretary to his paralegal, and then to his wife, and they moved in together, I saw a paper peel-off name tag, the kind worn at a business convention, in their master bathroom: *Brenda Troisi*. Since it had already been used and was stuck to the windowsill of the bathroom, I figured it was trash. When I asked Brenda if she wanted me to throw it away, she said, "Are you kidding? Don't you dare. I worked long and hard for that name." Her face reddened, and she stared at me with her cutting features: her sharp nose, her high, prominent cheekbones, the bulging whites of her eyeballs.

When my parents were still married, she was Brenda Smith, the secretary with the blonde feathered hair and the light laugh, who told me jokes while I watched her long, painted nails fly across the keyboard. She was the secretary my father sent in his place when he was supposed to have shown up at my swim team practices; at five years old, huffing in the pool, I'd look to the bleachers, scan the adult faces, and see her smile, flashing her straight, white teeth.

I mulled over Brenda's words, "worked long and hard," thought about what she might be referring to—offering to walk me down the road to get a vanilla swirl cone when my mother and I visited the office, ringing our home phone off the hook, sitting on my father's desk in a miniskirt, legs uncrossed in hopes of seducing him. She stomped out of their bedroom, and I watched glimpses of Brenda Smith disintegrate into nowhere. I knew that I was now faced with Brenda Troisi, a woman with incalculable dimensions, a woman with a look that pierced, and a voice that penetrated the way Alex Forrest's did in *Fatal Attraction*, when she said, "I am not going to be ignored."

*

Brenda pulled clothes from her closet and imitated the "wire hanger" scene in *Mommie Dearest*, where Faye Dunaway played Joan Crawford, the mother who woke her daughter up to beat her with hangers in the middle of the night. Brenda flung outfits down on the bed, squeezed hangers out of neck holes, loosened clips from waistbands of pants and skirts. She twisted the hooks of the hangers to show how easily they bent, and looked at me with her frantic smile, her wild eyes lost in their white spaces. She asked, "Imagine having a stepmother like *that*?"

Even though Brenda implied that she was joking, with her too, you were always in trouble without understanding why. You put the towel back on the rack the wrong way; you rolled your eyes; you didn't smile enough in front of the company; you were getting too fat or too skinny; you made the wrong sound or sigh when she was in the wrong mood. When I mustered up the courage to say I'd rather stay home instead of visiting one weekend, she became a ventriloquist, whispering to my father while he yelled: "You ungrateful little bitch. When you're twenty-five, you'll realize what an asshole you're being."

*

Each weekend before my father picked me up from my mother's house, in order to hide my crying, I stood in front of the bathroom mirror and doused my eyes with Visine. I studied the creases in my forehead, the tightness of my mouth, while I waited for the redness to dissipate. I dreaded visiting his and Brenda's split-level house with the back deck overlooking the pool, the hammock swinging from the oak, the neatly landscaped lawn.

I knew that most parents didn't call their kids "disgusting," didn't say, "The longer you sit the wider your ass spreads," or "You deserve nothing," and then take them shopping for school clothes. I knew that most parents didn't make their kid sleep in a closet, that they didn't coat these actions with the words, "It's like your own special room, nice and cozy." When I was at their house, Brenda said, "It's a beautiful day out—let's take a ride together—just you and me," which really meant that she'd drive us to the red house on nearby Locust Street, where a man murdered his wife. "You never really know what someone is capable of, no matter how much you might think you know them." I stared at the house as if it was something I'd seen in a horror movie, wondering if and when she'd drive us away from it, wondering if this is what Joan Crawford meant when she defined her parenting philosophy as *discipline mixed with love.*

*

Brenda talked about sending my sisters and me away all the time—"getting rid of us." Since my sisters weren't there, I knew that she was only talking about me. I remembered her words while we watched the television movie, *Small Sacrifices*, starring Farrah Fawcett—as she shot her three kids.

"What a sicko," Brenda said, and turned up the volume. I kneeled on the living room carpet and played solitaire, slow to flip each card over. Red, then black, then red. My insides tensed up. I tried, as I always did during these visits, to let time slip by me.

Duran Duran's "Hungry Like the Wolf" blared through Farrah's speakers as the gunshots sounded. Pow! Pow! Pow! One, two, three. I wanted to shudder, but I didn't. I kept my eyes on the cards, focusing on the queen of hearts, the dusty carpet, anything but the television. "Did you see that, Gina? This is a true story. It happened out in Oregon."

"Yeah, I know. I think I heard that." My stomach ached, twisted as if it was being wrung out, as if my organs were constricted by my flesh, suffocated by my skin.

"I love this song. One of my favorites of all time." Brenda went on, mentioned that the movie was based on a book describing this incident, said that this was Farrah's best acting job yet, but her voice faded. I pretended to listen. I looked up and nodded between her sentences. The music dulled into a faint hum in the background, and the sound of her voice muffled. I was becoming skilled at censoring what I heard, wrapping myself with an invisible film that no one from the outside could detect. I had no bruises, no bite marks or broken bones, but I endured the pain until my body tingled, until I became numb.

*

When I was five, I saw *The Shining* with my father. I watched Jack Nicholson play Jack the writer, a man who took a job at a resort in the Colorado mountains and tried to murder his family. For years I'd remember the haunting of the twin girls, the chilling drone of the trombones, the half-human, half-dead ghost emerging from the shower to seduce Jack, and I'd run from the bathroom to my bedroom screaming. I saw my wide eyes and quivering legs in the mirror at the end of the hallway. I saw the terror of an image exploding behind me, chasing me.

My sisters and I heard rumors that *The Shining* was filmed at The Balsams, a resort in northern New Hampshire where we learned to ski, where as a family we went on vacation each year. And where my parents, one New Year's Eve, told us that they'd decided to take a break from their marriage. I stood by the king-sized bed, my head its same height, while my mother explained that they were going to live apart, maybe try out dating one another for a while. Her face filled up with grief while my father painted himself with indecision, as if an actor unsure about which persona to develop: *the worried father, the apathetic father, the disappearing father.* I was too young to comprehend what this news meant for my sisters and me, distracted by the notion that my parents would date again, transport themselves back to younger versions of the single selves they no longer recognized.

*

During the years when I was nine, then ten, then eleven, my mother picked me up from my father and Brenda's house each Sunday evening at five-thirty. At four-thirty I planted myself in front of the picture window overlooking the driveway and waited for her to arrive. I stood there and grabbed onto the sheer white curtain, stared through the glass at the pavement, at the rows of hedges lining the driveway, at the front lawn. I watched and I waited, opened and shut my eyes as if they were cameras snapping pictures of my future. Even though my mother was always late, lost in a hectic space of work and cooking and tending to the needs of a household with three daughters on her own, I convinced myself that she would never make it—that we'd be doomed with her car crashing on her way to pick me up. I saw flashes of her white Honda wrapped around a tree, her limbs twisted. I saw myself standing over her coffin, floating ghost-like above her.

I trembled as the clock ticked, as the sky darkened. I choked back the mucus in my throat. I could relate to Jack's son in *The Shining*, to the way he was uncertain about what was happening inside his mind, to his fear of going crazy, his obsession with images of the dead twin girls and blood sloshing down hallways. Week after week, I gasped, trying to steady my breath as tears fell onto the carpet, as I feared becoming lost in limbo, stuck swimming in the purgatory of my father and Brenda's space. In these moments, the moments when I became fixated with death, I sensed that things were terribly wrong in the same way Jack's son did when his father said, *I would never hurt you.*

*

When I was thirteen, my uncle died from a heroin overdose. He was six years younger than my father. During my early years, he splashed with us in the pool in my grandparents' backyard, flipped barbecue meat on the grill, dated a woman, Nikki, who waitressed at the 99 Restaurant in town, whom I grew to love. Once, when I was four or five, and my sisters and I were walking down the street, some neighborhood kids stole my doll's shoe. My sisters dragged me back to my grandparents' house, crying, and we told my uncle the story. When we finished, he didn't say anything, just climbed onto his motorcycle and flew down the road. Minutes later, he returned, his hair wild as he slid into the driveway, held the small shoe up in the air, and grinned.

Days after he died, Brenda kneeled on the floor of the living room and rifled through his things. She read his credit card bills aloud. "I bet Chinese food is really good when you're high." She dumped out boxes of his Harley gear, his clothes and watches scattered on the floor like garbage. She shoved his black leather cap in my face, and said, "You want to know what pot smells like?"

I already knew what pot smelled like. I was relieved by the sweet smell of the leather cap, transported to the backs of cars filled with friends with whom I smoked joints and blunts and took bong hits each day after school. At night I waited outside convenience stores asking men to buy me booze, and they did. When no one was around to buy it, I stole—cheap wine and cigarettes, along with lip gloss and clothes. Soon, I'd stop drinking and start dropping acid, mistake fireworks for fire. I'd decide that I'd rather hallucinate—stare at oaks swaying in the breeze, become mesmerized by their enormity— than do anything else. It was only in these moments after I'd eaten bits of chemical-coated paper that I was able to care about nothing but the trees; when I was high, the oaks and pines turned into redwoods before my eyes, branches contorted like limbs about to wrap themselves around me, tuck me into the nooks of their trunks, cradle me from the wind, save me somehow.

Brenda tossed items into a small trash can, blurted random remarks. "What a fucking loser." I said nothing, even though my favorite uncle had died. Even though I suspected that I was not unlike him.

Brenda and I followed our script to the letter—she the overbearing, malicious stepmother, and me, the quiet, troubled teenager—executed our parts as if we'd rehearsed them. My voice was soft: "Can I look through that box? In case I want something in there?"

She pulled the box toward her as if she had been

appointed power of attorney, but instead of handing it over, she said, "You can have the cap," and picked it up off the floor to toss it to me. I tried not to flinch as it dropped onto my lap. I grabbed the hat, held it by the rim, felt the coldness of its worn inside, touched the orange embroidered logo. I didn't look at Brenda. I accepted my role. I was as solid as a statue, as predictable as a porcelain figurine behind the glass doors of their dining room hutch.

*

Because my father was a lawyer who argued for a living, and my mother had lost various battles to him over the years, when I expressed my misery about going to his house, she told me I'd have to go to court, stand in front of an actual judge, plead my case. "He won't listen to me," she said. "I'll never win."

At my father and Brenda's house, in the bedroom with the detached bunk beds and plain tan walls, a bedroom I had never moved into, I kneeled on the carpet in front of the full-length mirror. I pulled my neck upright, stuck my chest out while I rehearsed my lines: *I don't want to come here anymore. I don't think I should have to come here anymore. Please, don't make me come here anymore.* I muttered these words. I studied the curves of my lips in the mirror as I released them in whispers. I widened my eyes, narrowed my eyes, tried to release the furrow between my brows, but it wouldn't go away. I closed my mouth, frowned, half smiled. I stood up and made gestures with my hands: rested them on my hips, closed them into fists, clasped them and let them hang down in front of me. *The serious daughter. The assertive daughter. The sad daughter.*

I had tried this before. I had measured my father and Brenda's moods, waited for the best possible times to talk to them, but it was always the same. I developed a stutter, became flustered by the heat of blood in my neck, my jaw, distracted by the sound of my pulse. My palms perspired and my head pounded. I avoided their eyes as I uttered words, making up bits about getting older, about wanting to hang out with friends more. No matter how I phrased this, their response was always the same, despite a few words tweaked here and there. Brenda held her glass of pink wine, her face without a trace of emotion, while my father yelled. "You are so fucking selfish. You appreciate nothing."

"It's not her fault, Joe," Brenda said. "She's her mother's robot."

I stood in front of them on the border of the kitchen and living room, the step up to the hardwood floor giving me height. He kept going: "Oh, I know. Your mother and her three bears." I shrank.

Each time in the mirror, while I deciphered who I should be, I hoped that this time would be different. That I'd muster up the courage to say what I never did: that I could not bear to visit my father and Brenda's house any longer, that I thought of the two of them as twisted characters in the horrific movies we'd watched, that this was the only way I'd been able to make sense of them. What I did not say was that I had become a person who stood outside of myself and looked inward, that I could not continue this pretense, that I had ridden the waves of these turbulent visits for so long that I'd been gutted of who I was before ever piecing myself together; I was now utterly lost, searching for blueprints of who I would have been.

In front of the mirror, I was unrecognizable, a mass of anxieties wrapped up in skin, hidden behind eyes. I was Christina Crawford, who, unable to take it any longer, fought back when her mother strangled her, who finally spoke the unspeakable when she asked her mother why she ever wanted her in the first place. I was Alex Forrest, who knew what she wanted, who wouldn't take no for an answer. I was Jack's son, running through a labyrinth of snow-covered hedges, looking for a way out.

*

When my father was indicted for fraud, he said he had to tell me something. I had no idea what it was. I sat across from his desk in his office like a client bracing myself for news of a maximum sentence. He explained that he was being accused of mortgage fraud even though he was innocent, that if he was convicted he'd be facing jail time. His face was grave. His eyes teared up. I didn't wonder whether or not he was telling the truth; I was indifferent. I sat stone-like, unable to feel anything for his pending situation, for circumstances that could change everything for him.

I had watched my father slide in and out of various roles without a thought: *the husband, the adulterer, the lover*. I had never known him. To me he could have been anyone or nobody, the lines on his face and hands tracing back to a reality we had never shared. The distance between us prevented the possibility of this scene; I was not sure what he wanted here, but I guessed it was a dramatic moment between the two of us. Because I knew what was expected of me, I played the role of the sad daughter—the worried and concerned daughter. "I'm sorry," I said. I imagined what someone else, a girl who was afraid of losing her father to prison might do or say, but I, the girl who felt relieved by the thought of my father's absence, was hollow. We sat in silence while he looked at me, his head tilted, his face waiting.

"I'm sure it will be okay," I said.

*

In my twenties, I dated a man who was still living with his ex-girlfriend. I was living nowhere, so we had sex on the bathroom floors of friends' apartments. We moved from floors to counters, bath mats to showers. One of these times, after we stripped one another, he called me his ex's name by accident, and I got over it rather quickly, more easily than I expected from myself. Even though I was in love with this man, a man similar to my uncle, a man who had a magnetic personality and an addiction to heroin, I was not upset for more than a moment. I was his ex; I was myself—what was the difference? He and I were bound by a common need to escape ourselves; together we shed our skin again and again. I'd become used to alternate realities. I was used to trees talking, yellow lines swerving in the wrong directions along roads, people cropping up like ghosts, and disappearing. I was used to being disappointed, then elated.

When he called me her name, it echoed off the bathroom walls, dissolved into these moments we had together. It was overridden by the way I fulfilled what this man desired, by the way he believed he'd get clean for me, by the way I was convinced I could help him kick his habit. I expected I could be both his ex and myself—both the addict and the savior. In these moments, it didn't matter that I knew our union would not end well, that I would not be able to help or keep him, that I would not be able to let go of him.

*

I have only one photo from the stretch of years spent with my father and Brenda. We are in Montreal. I am almost in the sixth grade. I look skinny and pale, as I have stopped eating most days. My white t-shirt is tucked neatly into my pleated shorts, and I am wearing white sneakers and socks. My long hair is curled, my bangs a perfect puff, and I'm sitting on a stone wall next to Brenda, my leg propped up, my chin in my hand, smiling. One would never know that this girl wasn't happy to be on this family vacation, that she refrained from ever speaking her thoughts or mind, that she had made an extreme effort to become this thin, to begin to fade away. There would be no way to know that each Friday, when the girl's father drove her to the doctor so she could prove that she was gaining weight, she convulsed, cried to the point of hyperventilating the way Christina Crawford did when her mother doused the bathroom floor with a white cleaning powder and screamed at her daughter to, "Clean it up!"

I once read an interview with Christina Crawford, conducted just after she released *Mommie Dearest*, the book that the movie was based on, where the reporter mentioned that the walls and mantle in her house were absent of photographs, that it was like entering a place where there was no indication of time. I imagined that she saw no point in framing a version of herself on a carousel, wearing a pink dress and flashing a huge smile, when, just beyond the periphery of the snapshot, she'd see the truth— her mother cutting off her hair in a drunken rage, or making her stay at the dinner table until she'd eaten all of her raw steak. I imagined she refused to remember the way she'd seen things split open, pieces broken and jagged before falling away, before becoming lost.

*

A couple of years after I graduated from high school, my father told me that he was at the commencement ceremony. That he sat by himself in the rain, saw me receive my diploma, then left. I imagined him, his head covered with a baseball cap, the scorned father in the bleachers. That perhaps he expected people would see him there, crushed from his recent divorce, a speck in the crowd of families—parents and siblings, aunts and uncles grouped together, huddled underneath umbrellas. *The lonely, rejected father.* This was several years after the fraud charges against him had been dropped, but only a couple of years after he called to say that Brenda was trying to take all of his money, half of his business—right around the time when he expected pity again, and I played the part of the caregiver who should have felt compassion, but could not.

*

All through my twenties and thirties, I worked as a bartender. I got paid to act. To feed people booze and food, assess their needs, give them what they came in for, all the while shielding myself from their hungriest, often times ugliest sides. My co-workers and I listened, joked, flirted—feigned interest in people's lives. We deciphered their gestures, adjusted our tones of voice, mended their moods. We accommodated by adapting to different temperaments and personalities. We tried to make their pain subside. The job came naturally to me; in many ways, it was easy.

One night after work, I went out for drinks with one of my regular customers, Bob. We talked about drugs—about him having never touched them—about me getting too far into them—about the men I've loved, particularly the one similar to my uncle, and about Bob's successful marriage to his high school sweetheart.

"I'm so disappointed," he said. "I can't believe you've done drugs, dated an addict. You're ruining it for me. My wife and I always thought you were such a prude."

On the other side of the bar, in alcohol-induced euphoria or sadness, patrons painted our lives— labeled us prudes or sluts, loud or quiet, sane or insane, and we stepped into these roles for them— we fulfilled their fantasies. After all, it was they who paid us. We paid in other ways.

We tried not to let customers degrade us, but they often did, and in most cases, it was unacceptable for us to say so. We maintained composure even when the environment was stressful. We showed no anger. It was in this business that people often said to me, "You are the happiest person I know." But I was not—I was just doing my job. Sometimes I said this, but most times I nodded, smiled in response to these remarks that set me up for a standard I would never reach. It was like being on stage or screen, what happened next prompted by our attempts to fill existing molds. I found myself once again unwavering, a ceramic fixture afraid of breaking.

When I mulled over Bob's words, I gathered that my ability to adapt wasn't as essential as theirs on the other side—that loss is more prominent for those holding the illusions, those facing the realization that a person is not who they hoped she'd be. It is human to gravitate toward what we want to believe—it is similar to the way we decide to deny or ignore death, the way its reality changes what we know about life. I like to think that I am no longer afraid to die, that I no longer have illusions.

*

When I watch movies, I react as if they are real. I scream, gasp, tremble. I have to get up and leave the room. My boyfriend, Derek, says, "It's only a movie— why do you have that worried look?" It's become a joke between us. He reminds me that "these people are actors," that it is "only a job."

When we re-watched *The Shining* in the middle of the day, our curtains open and the light spilling in, I made myself sit through the entire movie. The memories of scenes flashed before me: Jack's son foaming at the mouth after he had a murderous vision, Jack's wife screaming as he chased her with an ax. During the bathroom scene, the one that haunted me for years, I shuddered as the beautiful woman transformed, as her smooth skin became covered with sores, as she became a skeleton. The difference between watching it now as opposed to then, is that I know what to expect. I am able to distance myself in a way that I couldn't when I was a kid. I am not six or seven or eight trying to tiptoe through Brenda's house, slip through rooms without her noticing, sneak outside to circle the neighborhood, pluck dandelions from people's yards. I'm not creeping into the shed in the backyard looking for a place to hide.

When *The Shining* ended, I got up, went into the bathroom and looked in the mirror. I studied my reflection, pouted my lips, tried to figure out what Derek means by the "worried look," something he mentions often, but I have never seen. It fascinates me that we don't know the language of our own faces—the expressions we make unconsciously, but never see ourselves—how it is up to others to construct their meanings, their purposes.

I heard Derek call to me from the living room. "Are you done watching scary movies for a while?" I turned on the faucet, let it run for a moment. The water filtered the silence. I studied the image of the person in the glass, contemplated the lines of the skin, as she looked back at me and nodded.

Part II:
Nowhere Else
But Here

In the Absence
of Beauty

When my sister, Krista, telephoned about Nanu's hospital admission, I was twenty-three years old. "Gina," she said. "I'm glad I caught you. It's important."

My grandmother had died a couple of years earlier, and Nanu was alone in the dark bedroom when he woke up, gasping for air. He reached for the nightstand and dialed 911 with his half-crippled fingers.

When she called to tell me this, I was kneeling in my bedroom in New Hampshire, an hour north of my hometown, stuffing t-shirts and long skirts into my duffel bag, in the midst of packing my truck to drive down to the west coast of Florida, where Nanu lived. He told me he'd been preparing for my arrival—filling the cupboards with Rice Crispies and gallons of Carlo Rossi wine, and stocking the freezer with homemade lasagna.

I was not only going to Florida to visit Nanu, but I was on my way to Panama City Beach to live and apprentice with Ursula, my herbalist and friend. Ursula aided me when I made the decision to give up drugs a few years before; she prescribed roots and tinctures, loaded me up with capsules and herbs. I had finished my degree in English Literature four months before, had been waiting tables and bartending in a nearby restaurant while living on Birch Street with my four closest friends with whom I laughed, drank kegs of beer, and played ping pong while the music blared until the early morning.

It felt right that I was leaving then, after college, to start a new life. It was 2002, the year after the World Trade Center terrorist attack, a summer of conflict about whether the United States should invade Iraq, and an anonymous neighbor had placed a rock inscribed with the word *hope* in our front yard. I believed this, like everything else, to be a sign.

*

When Krista called about Nanu, she said, "They think it's his gallbladder, but they've admitted him because they want to do some tests. They've ruled out cancer, so it shouldn't be too much to worry about."

But why would his gallbladder make him lose his breath? I couldn't imagine how alone he had been, how afraid.

For a man who wore an ACE bandage after falling off his bike, but lied to us and said, "This? This is an old football injury," I knew that if it wasn't for the loss of breath, he'd be trying to mend himself at home under his own supervision. He had never been admitted to a hospital before.

When I called room twenty-four, a hoarse voice answered. It sounded like his vocal cords were shredded, like uttering a simple word was unbearable. "Nanu."

"Hi, GG."

"I'm leaving to come down tomorrow," I said.

"GG, it really isn't a good time. I won't be at the house. I'm really sick."

"I still think I should come. I can watch the house, and I'll come stay with you at the hospital until you're back on your feet. Besides, who's going to eat all that food?"

"No, it really isn't a good time, GG." I could barely make out his slow, scarce words. *Who was this person on the other end of the phone with laryngitis? How was he so sick, when he'd been fine? When was the last time I'd heard from him?*

I felt bad keeping him on the line—it sounded like hot tea was scorching his throat. I said, "Okay, I love you. Talk to you soon."

But I was still going to Florida. I was not going to let the man I loved most in the world be alone in a hospital, listening to vague test results from disorganized doctors.

*

The driving was meditative. By the time I'd driven out of New England—through New York City and D.C., the highway lined with pines and hemlocks, the day clear with sunshine—I was finally relaxed. I was able to forget my perpetual restlessness, my uneasiness. I thought about what Nanu and I might do for the next few weeks, after he recovered. Maybe we'd go for a hike by the coast, me insisting that he hand over the lawn chairs, and him refusing to let me carry them. Maybe I'd sit on the screened-in porch and edit some old poems while he painted, duplicating a nature photo, or a graphic he'd printed off the computer. Or maybe a harbor cruise would suit us, one where we could gamble, like we'd been doing more and more since he'd grown too tired to take care of his own boat.

By the time I reached the Smoky Mountains of North Carolina, the gray mist interspersed with light, I felt worlds apart from the life I had been leading—I had just said goodbye to a new love, John. It was the type of affair one must leave just as it begins, mostly because that's what it felt like—an affair, as he had only recently broken up with his girlfriend, whom he still lived with, and I knew things weren't finished between them. Also, I'd been avoiding asking about the drug problem I knew he had. I had been obsessed for weeks, even months—obsessed with his hair's waves and the freckles on his shoulders, the surface of his skin. I had been obsessed to the point of distraction at the restaurant where we worked, fumbling up orders, bringing customers wrong meals, and spilling drinks at tables. My obsession had been boiling over into other parts of my life, like when the phone rang, and I hoped it was him, and when it wasn't I still heard his voice in my head while trying to have a conversation with someone else. Like a new and exciting career, this affair had been all-consuming. Like a narcotic, it had numbed me for a while.

I cruised along the curves, weaved in and out of the mountains. The trees stood bold against the charcoal drizzle. The fog stilled the air around the red and silver maples. I wondered about my Nanu's older sister, Christina, who lived somewhere around these woods. He'd tell me, "My sister lives there," at even the slightest mention of the Smokies. "It's beautiful." As my truck meandered around the rolling hills, climbing up and gliding down, I heard CDs and backpacks and books roll around in the cab of the truck.

More trees—striped maples and mountain maples. The cell phone on the passenger seat rang, sounding like tambourines. It took me by surprise, since I'd borrowed it from a friend for emergency purposes. I picked it up.

"You better just turn around." Krista's voice was feverish, her sobs loud.

"What?" I lowered Paul Simon's "Graceland" playing on the stereo.

She steadied her voice. "Nanu's dying," she said, finding breaths in between her words. "They gave him two weeks to live. It's cancer of the esophagus."

What was she talking about? This was absurd, unbelievable, and definitely some sort of mistake. "Slow down, Krissy. What are you talking about?"

"The doctors are saying he has one of the worst cases of esophageal cancer they've ever seen. He must have been sick for a while and keeping it a secret ... you'd better just turn around. Dad is flying him up to New Hampshire to die." A secret? What was this? How could Nanu have known? *I won't be at home, GG. I'm very sick.*

I couldn't hear her anymore. A piercing sound flooded my ears, its tones creeping up each side of my head. I remembered Nanu talking about having to eat foods with less flavoring the last couple of months because of heartburn. It had seemed normal for an eighty-two-year-old who'd been eating tomato sauce and drinking red wine his entire life. That was the only thing that had been out of the ordinary, besides the less frequent phone calls, but were they even less frequent? With my recent infatuation and my move, I'd been neglecting our Sunday phone calls, which I usually depended on.

It was twilight, carnation pink hiding behind blue-gray clouds. The clouds stretched across the sky, wedging in between layers of the universe, he and I falling like microscopic drops of ink on the earth's canvas. Fading. I thought back to our last annual visit to Florida. It was on Thanksgiving, which was also my birthday. Nanu was equipped with a bottle of sparkling Korbel Brut, and we clanged champagne glasses in celebration of the new year ahead. He'd told all his friends in the old folks' park, "My granddaughters are coming to visit. One of them is a rebel (Krista), and the other one's a hippie (me)." He and I debated about herbal medicines and shared thoughts on Christianity. Although Nanu spent his life working with his hands, the owner of his own plumbing company, he was an avid reader, and we discussed his findings, from prostate health to the origin of the world. From Adam and Eve to Darwin. From Nazi Germany to Bin Laden. As usual, he told me to relax, to ease up on my perpetual paranoia, my concerns about toxic tap water, and to live more like him, without worries. A wonderful idea, but impossible for me to do. Krista and I joked with him about it over salad with blue cheese crumbs, homemade sautéed greens, and pizza.

Nanu was open-minded for an old man. He supported my participation in pro-abortion rallies in Washington D.C. "Women should make the choice when it comes to their own bodies." He encouraged road trips across the country, and my decision to take time off after high school to think about whether or not I wanted to go to college. "Just another experience. I think that's wonderful, GG," he'd say in response to my idea to drive further, to see more ground, when friends and family members insisted my notions were poorly thought out and unrealistic—that I'd never go to college if I didn't go right away, and that I was wasting time working in restaurants. "Maybe you'll be like Naomi, and become a manager," Nanu said about my boss, whom I admired.

*

After hanging up with Krista, I dialed the hospital again. I wanted to tell Nanu that the Smokies were every bit as beautiful as he'd described. "There are wildflowers everywhere. I think they've just bloomed. And I drove by a waterfall in just the right light. It's a little paradise."

"Okay, GG. I'm glad you're there."

"I'll see you soon. I'm on my way back home. I love you."

*

I stopped at a campground in Ashville and set up my tent by a winding river. Taking my time to gather branches, I started a small fire. I smoked cigarettes while drinking a large Heineken by the light of the flames. And cried. My body carried far too much weight. It felt strapped to the ground, as if in a straitjacket. I played solitaire for a while, and tried to feed myself spoonfuls of peanut butter, but it was useless. No hunger visited, not the physical kind. The rushing river soared through the trees, ripping through mossy branches—I lost myself to the sound. For moments, I heard nothing else, not even my own thoughts.

It was late, but I couldn't sleep, so I stayed sitting on the dirt watching logs form bridges across the water. Sitting with the birches in the mountains by the river, I wondered if Nanu was lying awake in the hospital on an uncomfortable bed, in a room with white walls. I thought about how he was at peace in the woods, how he needed to see this place where I sat and to feel its magic, even though I could not. Scraping my sneakers against the dirt I made shapes, thinking about how my life had intersected his, how our piles of memories were made up over time, how the absence of my father, his son, had deepened our union, had fed it and fueled it. I thought about how even though he'd served in the Navy, he never talked about the war, how no one did, but instead he spoke of Hawaii, of Japan, of his travels during that time. I remembered his strength when dealing with his younger son, my uncle, Dicky—how Nanu used his savings to send him to rehabs, to bail him out of jail, and then how he pretended not to be crushed when it turned out to be for nothing. I thought about John, an addict—someone's father and someone else's son, and how I wanted him near me now. Sitting, I cradled my knees until the sun rose.

When day broke, I crawled back into the tent to nap. I finally fell asleep, but Nanu visited my dreams, stumbling over words he couldn't pronounce. He was trying to talk to me, to tell me something. Attempting to respond, I'd open my mouth, but each time I discovered I lost my voice. In sleep, my vocal cords severed, and my lungs lost their breath. In sleep, panic barged in.

*

My father, who I hadn't talked to in years, was going to be flying Nanu up to New Hampshire. Nanu was being taken to my father's house, despite the fact that he never wanted to leave Florida, where he golfed and boated, painted landscapes and portraits on his screened-in porch. He was being taken to my father's house on a lake, filled with a family I'd never met, and a woman, Dawne, I'd only seen once from afar—she had long Barbie-like hair and a slender figure. What would my sisters and I do there, seeing Nanu for his last days and breaths?

My life seemed to stretch along the highway like a path I'd keep following until it dropped off the earth. I was moving to Florida, but Nanu wouldn't be there any longer. I wanted to pour him a glass of wine and wake him up from this staggering sickness. Outside the moon was almost full. Shimmers of silver flashed across the windshield. I saw his golden brown eyes. I saw the ambulance. And surges of red. Red, streaking like lightning.

I pushed north on Interstate 95. I drove from state to state for sixteen hours, stopping only to use bathrooms and buy cappuccinos from sticky convenience store machines. I drove until I reached my mother's house in New Hampshire, until my eyes were red and swollen, until my neck was stiff with exhaustion. When I arrived, it was late at night, and I collapsed in the guest bedroom, sleeping through the entire next day.

*

Dawne, Krista, and I stood nervously at the gate inside the airport. Dawne's profile reminded me of

Brenda's, the sharp cheek bone structure and the triangular nose. Her clothes were looser—she wore a long linen dress that belled out beneath her breasts. She was fair, with sky blue eyes and only a touch of makeup. "Are you girls close with him?" she asked.

"Yes." I couldn't speak any further. I scanned the people, trying to halt my whirling thoughts. *How did he handle this torturous plane ride? Was he scared?* I was terrified.

There was my father. He looked aged, with more wrinkles than I remembered, his face having lost its symmetry. He pushed a wheelchair, too quickly it seemed, his feet fumbling beneath him. In the chair, an old man I didn't recognize. He was skinny, almost emaciated, his face sunken in so deep that his eyeballs bulged. His clothes hung from his shrunken figure. His fingers shook as if he'd just undergone electric shock treatment. His hands didn't look like his. I knew them as thick and darkened by sun, with strong tendons from years of physical work. They were small now, his fingers shriveled and dry and old, so old. His face wore an expression between pain and fear, as if he was in too much pain to be scared and too scared to feel the pain. If I didn't know this was my Nanu, I might have thought he was a concentration camp victim who'd just been released but had no hope of survival. I couldn't hide my shock. I'd never seen death this close.

He didn't say hello and neither did we. We were still like trees on a windless day. "I have to pee," he said.

"Okay, okay," my father responded. They'd done this before. "He has to pee," he said, with a quick glance at us. We nodded, our bodies motionless, soundless. He wheeled Nanu around the corner into the restroom. His motions were automatic, but his face looked flustered, and he sounded winded. I couldn't even imagine him assisting Nanu in a bathroom stall—a man who had three children, but probably never changed a diaper or fed an infant a bottle, ever.

Krista looked at me. "Oh my God," she said, her mouth wide.

*

On the way back from the airport, the car filled with flustered small talk, mostly from my father, which I could barely hear. Krista stared at the highway, while I sank back into the leather seat and rested my head against the window. He mentioned that hospice people were coming to the house. There was conversation about a bed in a room. He was matter-of-fact, stating what we needed to know. I was looking at Nanu in the passenger side mirror while my father talked as if he wasn't even there, as if he were already gone. *This is what will happen. We won't ask you because you have lost your voice.* I wanted to talk to him, but I had no words, and I imagined that it was painful for him to talk. His pupils were dilated from the morphine. I'd never seen his eyes this wide open; they looked so large that I believed all he could see was death.

*

The dirt road to my father's house wound along the edges of a lake, like one you might take to a summer camp or cottage. The house was beige, a garage underneath a balcony overlooking the lake. I wondered who lived there. My father and Dawne had been married for about a year, and I knew she had daughters. I didn't know if they were grown or not, and I didn't ask. I didn't want Nanu to worry that Krista and I were as uncomfortable as he must have been about spending our last days together at this house.

My father, Krista, and I crouched around the wheelchair and lifted it up the front stairs and into the house. Each wheel had its own struggle; we had to turn the chair and tip it just so, without moving him too much. I didn't expect this—that he'd be unable to walk or move. We were doing our best to keep the chair steady, but we were clumsy, and I suspected that each shake was painful. When I didn't think it was possible for his eyes to grow wider, they did, this time with shame.

Once inside, my father wheeled Nanu into the bathroom again. Krista and I stood in the living room. "Make yourselves at home, girls," Dawne said. A piano sat in the corner, in front of the staircase, and I wondered if she played. The kitchen and living room formed one large room. The wallpaper was peach with white petunias, and black-and-white Ansel Adams prints ornamented the walls. Snow covered pines. A rose and driftwood. Yosemite in the summertime. The balcony was off of this room, with immaculate windows lining the front of the house. The sun glowed over the water.

Dawne dropped our bags in the master bedroom, where she had prepared a hospital-type bed. The bed was white, crisp, and sterile. There was nothing gentle or kind about it, no fluffy satin throw pillows or fleece blankets. The pillowcases looked icy and their crinkled edges drooped over the sides. *They're too big*, I thought.

Dawne motioned to Krista and me. She pointed to a small gold crucifix in between her thumb and pointer finger. "I'm sneaking this under his pillow," she whispered. I didn't understand why she was telling us this. I didn't know what approval she sought. She placed it between the sandpaper pillowcase and the fold-up cot. I watched her from across the room, battling my lips to stay closed, to drown her out. Nanu wasn't Christian, or even slightly religious. Who was she trying to console?

*

Bach's *Brandenburg Concerto* played on the stereo in the bedroom. Krista and I sat on the edge of the bed that was nearest him. Dawne called from the kitchen, offering us pizza, but we refused. I couldn't eat. Nanu wouldn't take water or food; how could I? This was a man whose mantra had been, "Eating and drinking are two of the finest things in life."

Nanu closed his eyes, and Krista and I reclined on the flowery bedspread. My father and Dawne busied themselves out in the living room. They were making plans for urns and ashes and undertakers. They'd told us we were welcome to "camp out" here for a couple of weeks. When I told my mother that I was going to bring my tent and set it up in the yard, she said, "No, Gina. I think they meant to 'sleep over,' not to bring your tent."

I watched the grooves in the ceiling. I tried to meditate while Nanu drifted off, but I only saw him grow sicker and sicker, swirling down into a pool of blackness. I missed him and he wasn't even gone. I missed him painting furiously to the very music we listened to, shaping a white seagull with its wings spread, shades of aquamarine water rippling across the canvas. Exquisite. I missed the two of us at sunset in Florida, at the dock by the canal. I recalled one of our last times there, when I was mesmerized by the sunset, its orange, glowing glare. "Don't ever look directly at the sun before it descends, GG."

"Really? I always do. I'm too impatient."

"You shouldn't. It's not good for your retinas." His face was serious, as if he'd use all the power in him to protect my eyes—my eyes that saw him as strong and able, not breaking as he was now. Not broken. I was twenty-two, but we held hands as if I were still three years old, as if he needed to be sure I wouldn't lose my vision. My bare feet squished into the damp mud. At the dock, we had nothing to say. Our silence spoke, and followed us here to this awful beige bedroom in New Hampshire.

Nanu lay on the white twin bed, his eyes half open, while Krista and I listened to my father and Dawne bustle around the kitchen. They talked about food, and about setting up a bedroom for themselves upstairs. They were taking care of laundry and paperwork and phone calls—things that go along with death.

A bucket rested on the bureau. In between bouts of sleep, Nanu held his head up, bile forcing itself up his esophagus. When we heard him begin to clear his throat, Krista and I jumped. I propped his shoulders up while she held the bucket. His shoulders were sharp and pointed. Our touches pained him, but if we didn't lift him, he'd choke.

Listening to Bach reminded me of my arrivals at Fort Myers airport, Nanu pulling up to the curb to greet me, reaching across the car to open the passenger door of his white Crown Victoria, the classical music blaring. The violins and flutes and cellos. Of how I'd throw my suitcase in the back and plop myself into the passenger seat and he'd press on the gas, the warm air rushing in, my hair becoming wild as we sped away. Of how he'd look at me. "Isn't this music beautiful, GG?"

"Yes," I'd say, and turn ahead to take in the palm trees. I'd keep my window down the entire way, and soak in the humidity, welcome the blast of heat, the fiery glow of sun.

But we weren't there any longer. We were here, in the absence of beauty.

*

During the waiting, my other sister, Lisa, walked in, tanned from the Arizona sun. She wore corduroy overalls and a tie-dyed tank top. She leaned down and kissed our grandfather on the cheek. "Hi, Nanu."

"Hi, Lis." He forced the words out of his mouth, each syllable scraping the back of his throat.

"Can I read to you from the Bible?" Lisa, a born-again Christian, went nowhere without her righteous book. Nanu, whose father became a Jehovah's Witness during his childhood, was an atheist. After his mother died from a brain tumor in her late twenties, his father began bringing the New Testament to the dinner table each night. His father would holler, pound his fists, and insist that his children believe in paradise. He'd demand that they believe in being chosen. "Why do you think I was dying to join the Navy?" Nanu often asked. After leaving home, he rejected organized religion, believing that once a person died, he or she lay in the ground for all eternity. We'd discussed this many times before.

"Sure, Lis," he whispered. Lisa began to read, while Krista and I looked at each other. We knew that Nanu wouldn't have us sit by him for days while he withered away. I imagined that he was petrified— his face a picture of the way young children and the elderly mesh, the way we become children again as we age, scared of first steps and loud, foreign noises, insecure about what life brings us next. Or where it will deliver us. My temples pulsed, my limbs weak. Cramps rode up my calves. I felt trapped, as he must have, as if I were about to fall over into a pit of flames. I wanted to stand up for Nanu against the enormous God in the sky.

I thought back to the day when I was about to speak in a Catholic church, at my grandmother's funeral, but my eyes watered and my voice shook and stuttered. The priest turned to me with an impatient face and said, "Well, if you can't do this..."

My Nanu, standing next to me, looked directly at him. "Hey, this is an empowered woman you're talking to."

*

Out in the kitchen, there was more mention of hospice. In the bedroom, we pretended not to hear. A priest. The names of a nurse. Tomorrow she'd be here, or the next day. I couldn't even imagine a tomorrow when today was filled with yelps and shivers and alkaline fluid. When today silence wrapped itself around us like a torn blanket in the cold winter. Nanu was uncomfortable, but he couldn't move. He was unable to leave, unlike me, prone to bolt at the slightest sight of trouble.

I turned up the knob on the stereo, and Chopin's notes ascended and then fell, settling somewhere between a storm and an idle day—containing vast differences, like a plane lifting serenely into the sky, and then, its crashing explosion. Lisa raised her reading voice. "The Lord is my strength and my shield..."

My father and Dawne entered the bedroom. Dawne reminded us to help ourselves to the fridge while we were there. She looked like she felt sorry for Krista and me; we were crying, still on the bed. Lisa still sat in a chair by Nanu's cot, reading aloud, her legs stretched out, sustained by the footrest. Nanu closed his eyes again. He'd been doing this for hours—opening his eyes, then closing them, then the bile.

My father walked into the bedroom. "Hey," he said, and Lisa stopped reading. "The hospice nurse will come over tomorrow, or the next day. She won't sleep here, but she'll help out most hours of the day." I hated that Nanu was like a mannequin in the room, that since he could no longer respond, no one talked to him, only around him.

My sisters and I nodded.

Nanu jerked his head. His head that had not moved for hours. "This is not going to be prolonged." The voice was loud despite its sparseness, his declaration so strong that Lisa dropped the book. "Did you hear me?" He was looking at my father—warning him, and comforting us. I broke. Krista broke. Even Lisa broke. I felt like I was five years old, a small child dropped off at the mall alone, her parents taking off down the road. I broke.

He looked at me, helpless, as if to say, *What do you want me to do, GG?* His skin tightened. *How could this be happening? We still had so much more to talk about.* I still needed his wisdom. Here I was, after bringing myself back from drugs and destruction, still plunging into pain, still in love with danger. Here I was, hoping that Ursula would cleanse and purify me—that by forcing myself out of the comfortable chaos my life had been constructed of, that by moving into the unknown, I'd somehow be absolved.

The morphine drove his eyes mad. With each moment in between, when he closed his eyes, I thought he'd surrender to death. This couldn't possibly go on for days, my sisters and me without words in this crowded bedroom. My father trying to get Nanu to take some dribbles of water, or some ice cubes, which he continuously refused.

*

It was two o'clock a.m. when Nanu mentioned the Virgin. It happened just after Krista looked at Dawne and my father, sitting in chairs against the wall. "You two should go to bed," she said. "Get some sleep. We can stay up with him."

"Okay. We'll be right upstairs. But I'll give him his pill first." My father struggled with Nanu, who didn't want to swallow, who didn't want to be touched. My father crushed the pill with his fingers, and fed bits of it in between Nanu's lips. "To kill the pain," he said. "Really, just take it." It was difficult to tell whether he'd swallowed it or not, but at least it was inside his mouth now. "Good night, Dad. Good night, girls." They left.

Nanu closed his eyes. "She's walking through the village."

"Who?" I asked.

"Mary. The Virgin. She's walking in between the rows of people."

Krista, Lisa, and I looked at one another. "She's there," he said, his eyes closed. I tried to imagine brick walls where the Virgin walked. I tried to imagine what he saw. I wondered what verses Lisa had been reading to him; I hadn't listened, not to the meaning of the words. I thought of Jerusalem, dirt roads and temples and cloaks.

Later, Lisa said she thought he was talking to Jesus. Later, I said he hallucinated from the morphine. Later, Krista forgot what he said.

His eyes were bottomless, inviting us into their emptiness. I didn't see the village or the Virgin. I saw a nook in his backyard, where daisies and lilies and tulips flourished. They were bright pink, yellow, red. Growing next to them were garlic, sweet green peppers, fresh basil. Red vine tomatoes, the best I'd ever tasted, sliced and spread across homemade toast. He tended to the garden, wearing a sunhat to protect his chestnut eyes. Now, his eyes deep as caves hollowed out his face, telling stories of World War II, of being stationed off the coast of Honolulu when the Japanese attacked Pearl Harbor. They told stories of my grandmother sending him photos of herself

wearing grass skirts and leis, and of him proposing
to her on the beach. They told the story leading up to
mourning a child lost to heroin, the only time I saw
him cry, loud and hard.

CLEANING HOUSE

N anu's yard was absent of its orange blossoms. The grapefruit trees sagged, flimsy and defeated, the grass browned, flattened against the ground. I climbed into the back of my truck to find an empty backpack. I hesitated over a maroon tent with rusted, broken poles sticking out, the smell of mildew lingering in the air beneath the cab. As I stepped out into a warm breeze, the palm trees began to flail in the yard.

When Krista and I walked into the house, I expected the place to smell like Nanu: just a hint of garlic, and fabric softener or Pepsodent, or the oils he used to paint on the porch. For a moment I expected sautéed collard greens and pita bread spread out on the counter, but instead, I saw empty sub wrappers and soda cans.

My father greeted us. We hadn't seen him since Nanu's death five months before. He held each arm out as if ready for a group embrace, but instead, he tapped the backs of our shoulders at the same time. It was the hello you get from a stranger. Our father's hugs had always been either too long and tight, or tenuous and undecipherable, like this one. "Hi guys. It's good to see you. How was the drive?"

Krista and I had just sped to Florida in three days from Santa Cruz, California, where I lived for the summer. We stopped only once in Tennessee to visit

Nanu's sister, Christina, who made us biscuits and pork with gravy.

"Not bad," I said. "Not too much traffic, at least." He turned back to the sink to fill a glass with water.

"Hi, Krista. Hi, Gina," Dawne said. She offered her hand, first to Krista and then to me. Her slender fingers clenched my palm.

Dawne's yellow hair hung down to her waist. This was only the second time I'd met her, but I could tell that she was different from Brenda, more eager and less showy. She wore a long, cotton housedress. Her skin was free of make-up. She looked pretty. Young. After meeting her for the first time, Nanu said, "Joey has never been too bright with women, but I couldn't find anything wrong with her."

"Take whatever you want, girls. We've put a good dent in the place already," my father said.

Cardboard boxes covered the kitchen counters. Crinkled newspaper edges poked out of boxes. Silver World War II collectible coins scattered across the dining room table.

*

Back in New Hampshire, I'd stayed in the bedroom for hours, sitting with Nanu's lifeless body. When it was time to leave, I had to physically peel myself up from a chair beside him, tear myself away from him, this man who was more of a father to me than my own. Ursula had called to say that it was no longer a good time for me to stay with her in Panama City, so I had found myself still planning to leave but without a destination. I had been to California a few times, and it had long coincided with the notion of hitting the road, of my destiny manifested—summers sprinkled with love and wildflowers, the fire-lit beaches surrounded by circles of drummers, a crescent moon burning through the blue hues of dusk as the sun set—it represented a kind of communal life that I'd first discovered in San Francisco when I'd stayed for a month in a friend's dorm room after I finished high school, a life that I'd always been drawn to. Despite all of this, this time, when I'd decided to go to California, it was with the idea of being alone. After years of distraction, with drugs, and men, and booze, I felt I had no other choice.

After Nanu died in New Hampshire, I saw John a few more times, said goodbye to him again and again. From the moment we'd met, John's presence was familiar. I had the sense that we'd met before— that mildly disturbing feeling you get when you know a person from somewhere, but you can't quite place how—it seemed I'd heard his distinct voice deepen with rhythmic questioning, that I'd sensed his gray eyes penetrating me. I needed to know him more. Once I learned about his habit, about his addiction to the drug that people seldom quit, I left for California with the words of a close friend lingering in my mind: "You should never want something so bad that you can't walk away from it." I arrived in California torn between desire and will, staying and leaving, moving forward and looking back.

In Nanu's house, crystalline carved stem glasses stood tall behind the windowed cabinets. Endless jugs of Rossi red wine had filled these glasses, now empty. "Can I have these wine glasses?" I asked.

My father said, "I'm renting them out with the

house. I'm offering it fully furnished, so I want to keep the stuff in the cupboards here for the renters."

"Do you really think they need ten glasses?"

"Okay, you can take two."

I unloaded my backpack from my shoulders. Vertical creases ran up and down the glasses, the grooves spreading out at the bottom and expanding to create tiny diamond shapes. I slid my thumb over the divots, the glass shining like a prism on a south-facing windowsill. I cocooned the glasses in crumpled newspaper.

In the living room, paintings leaned up against the wall, stacked one behind the other below a wide rectangular mirror. At the end of our visits, Nanu encased the paintings in protective cardboard contraptions he tied together with string and sent us home with them, the makeshift boxes shielding the artwork during bumpy plane rides. When he was in the hospital, close to death, he said to Krista, "Krissy, you are in charge of the paintings. You and your sisters decide what to do with them."

Up until our last visit, one of his paintings hung on the wall in the hallway: on the canvas, twelve trees towered out of auburn soil, mud streaking near the roots in patches. Leaves curled under and touched one another like fingertips. In the background, grayish blue ocean rippled across land. Dark purple storm clouds rested on top of a setting sun. When I used to ask about it, Nanu would say, "That painting? That's an old one. That painting won an award." He'd study it for a moment and smile.

On our last visit to Nanu's house, we were celebrating my birthday with homemade ravioli and champagne. Still eating, Nanu stood up from the dinner table and approached the picture, fumbling with the hooks behind it.

"What are you doing?" I asked.

"I know you always wanted this," he said. "I'll pack it up for you."

"Are you sure?"

"I'm sure, GG. What am I going to do with it?" He turned to Krista and said, "I'll start painting you a duplicate of it."

She beamed. "You will?" She had asked about the painting weeks before he died.

"It's almost finished, Krissy," he said.

*

A small, framed picture of seashells hung on the wall:

Yesterday is history
Tomorrow is a mystery
Today is a gift
That's why we call it the present...

Nanu recited the first three lines of this saying on occasion, and my sisters and I clinked our glasses against his. For years I thought he'd made it up, but one day I saw the words and picture framed in a card store, so I mailed it to him.

When Nanu recited these lines, I believed he was trying not to think of my uncle, Dicky. As a child, I saw the inside of my uncle's bathroom minutes after he shot up, tiny drops of blood on the linoleum floor. I saw my uncle on heroin in the months before his death—the months when my mother would warn us not to answer the door to him when she wasn't home, no matter how much we might want to go for a ride on his motorcycle. I remember how relieved I was when he didn't stop by, so I wouldn't have to refuse to let him in, or be in trouble with her, since I knew I would never be able to keep the door closed. I saw him go back and forth for years, trying clinics and rehabs all over the country—living at these places so he might learn how to break free from his habit. I saw him when he was getting clean, relapsing, dying.

When Krista and I stopped in Tennessee and spent the evening with Aunty Christina, she spoke about how Nanu had been angry at the church because Dicky was molested by a Catholic priest, a teacher at his school, in the seventh grade. How Nanu numbed himself for years with scotch and red wine, how he refused to let himself feel the pain of it.

When Nanu recited the lines *Yesterday is history, Tomorrow is a mystery, Today is a gift,* I sensed that he was trying to accept everything about his life that he could not change. I was careful as I lifted the picture from the nail, gentle as I put it into my pack.

*

When Nanu died, I hadn't called John, but he'd heard through someone at the restaurant where we worked. I was back staying at the house on Birch Street with my friends from college, my truck still packed to move as I figured out where to go, what to do now that Ursula had changed her mind about my staying with her in Florida. The night he found out about Nanu, John let himself into my bedroom and tiptoed the path to my bed. It was dark in the room, and I'd been trying to sleep, but he didn't startle me.

I'd been expecting him. During the past weeks, I'd grown to assume his presence, although I tried not to admit this, even to myself.

John said, "I came to say I'm sorry. I've been thinking about you." He lit the lavender candle on my nightstand. He put a cigarette in his mouth and drew the flame of the candle to it, inhaling only enough to light it for me. When he passed it to my lips, I caught the tattoo of his son's name on the inside of his forearm: *Jacob*. This was the first physical detail of his that stood out to me on the day we met, one that, to me, said everything he hadn't. I had imagined how the needle carved his flesh, the letters forming, his skin tissue bubbling up as the ink was buried. In my bedroom, he studied my face and smiled with his mouth closed. He leaned his head closer to mine, his sand-colored hair brushing the nape of my neck.

I stared up at the ceiling and took a slow drag of the cigarette before turning all the way toward him. When I told him how alone I felt, how I'd never felt a distinct sense of home, but now I was utterly lost, he listened intently. He kept one hand underneath my shirt, on my stomach, his fingers rubbing my skin while he focused on my words.

"I felt like that when my mom died," John said. There was an ease in the way we talked, one that had been there since the day we met. He held my chin when we kissed, his full lips warming mine.

I knew that he was high that night—I could tell by the pink shadows outside his eyes, by the slow drawl of his voice, by his pin-sized pupils. I knew he could not get past the remembrance of his mother, who, in order to feed him, had turned tricks in their poor neighborhood while his father was in Vietnam. I knew that, for him, heroin was like oxygen for someone who cannot breathe. It helped him find a hint of hope.

The truth is, I was able to relate to John. I too moved in circles, repeated patterns, truly wanted to break out of the cycle I had created, the one where I learned difficult lessons over and over again. I, too, lived in a space between two worlds, the one where I tended to myself, and the one where I gave myself away. During my time in California, I had not let go. I had only tried to force myself to forget. I hiked through forests of redwoods and sequoias and meadows of lupines. I bought my food at farmers' markets, biked roads that curved along the sea, went to bars to hear live music alone and sober, listened to political speakers on street corners, even made a couple of friends. But all of this only took up space in between moments of staring out at the ocean and thinking about what I'd lost.

John moved his hand to my leg, to the inside of my thigh, his touch heating my skin. "I'm really sorry, Gina," he said again, his eyes unwavering while they searched mine.

*

In the living room, a picture of my sisters and me stood on a shelf above a cabinet. When we visited, Nanu would point, reminding us, "All the hard stuff's in there, girls." Glenlivet and Jack Daniels. Now, I polished off the dusty bottles with my shirt sleeve. I screwed the caps on tighter.

"Gina, how was California?" my father asked. His

voice was light, and he looked at me expectantly. I couldn't tell whether he was actually interested, or if his question was derived from nervousness, small talk to fill the silence.

"Great."

"Where to next?"

"I've been thinking about heading down to the Virgin Islands for a while, but nothing is set in stone. We'll see." In California, my house sublet had expired, and I was almost out of money. One of the friends I'd lived with back on Birch Street had suggested we save some money for a few months, then head to the islands for the winter, where we could find work in restaurants, but in reality, I didn't know where I was going, or what I was going to do next. I only knew that if I stayed in New Hampshire for long, I'd be compelled to stay with John.

I'd known the risks of becoming involved with an addict, although I'd ignored them, and I had the potential to ignore them again. I knew that John was imprisoned by his habit, but I saw an honesty in his struggle, a humanness that prevented me from wanting him to be anyone even slightly different than who he was. I saw the man who defended me when lunching businessmen made perverse comments about licking spilled vodka off my shirt, the man who cooked me a grilled zucchini and chicken dish and waited to walk me home at the end of his shift. I saw the man who I trucked miles with until we got to the woods, who planted himself next to me on rocks alongside the river, with whom I rolled up my pant legs and dipped my feet into the water to see how frigid it was. I saw the man who etched the name of his son into his skin.

My father said, "You know, one day you'll find that the most important journey is the one where you go inside of yourself instead of running away."

I ignored him.

I ignored him because since he left us years ago, he had only been concerned with his own journey—he had missed more sporting events, dance recitals, plays, concerts, and graduations than I was able to count. I ignored him because he didn't know me enough to deserve an explanation—we had never been close. I ignored him because I had been inside of myself the entire summer. In California, I spent sunsets running along the Pacific. I worked as a secretary for an art company by day. I wrote in the evenings, returning to stories and poems I had set aside years ago. I practiced yoga on the rocky cliffs by the ocean. I drank little, and quit smoking pot and cigarettes. I fed my juicer beets and kale daily. I abstained from sex, went to Dance Church on Sunday mornings. There, people of all races and religions gathered in a small, unfurnished studio with their old records. Paul Simon and Bob Marley spurred the movements of bodies. Some danced wildly, and some flowed with ease. I bowed to the altar dedicated to Buddha and Jah and Jesus. I tried to find God.

California was a place where I stepped out of time. I attempted to transform myself into who I was not, at least not yet—someone who rested and reflected, someone who paused to make sense of her choices. I had been born into dissonance, become accustomed to it, and once I found myself free from my father and Brenda, I dove into worlds without deliberating; I was easily drawn to a kind act, a soft voice, a gentle touch, never stopping to assess the depth of the water, how far I might float or flounder before possibly reaching the shore. I had become torn between wanting to roam free and the desperate desire to attach myself to something, to anything.

Before I left, John had said to me, "You're not like anyone I've ever met. You're so honest. And you have hope. You're not afraid." His face, lit up by candlelight, was close to mine, the spice of his breath mixed with our cigarette smoke. His voice lulled me as we pressed ourselves against one another.

This wasn't true. I did have hope, yes, had lived my entire life holding on to glimmers of it, looking for relief. But I was afraid of who I had become—uncomfortable in my own skin, fearful of my own company, the obsessive thoughts that rushed in. I became stricken by the thought of disappearing.

"I'm afraid of lots of things," I said. And I knew as I uttered these words, that I was afraid of losing him, of forgetting his tenderness, the way he listened, the way we knew one another so well for reasons both easily and not easily explained. In California, I tried to forget about my grandfather's death, and about John. But I could not forget either of them without forgetting myself.

I walked down the hall to my grandfather's bedroom. I crept into the closet and took inventory. I snatched two seventies-style neck ties off their hooks, and stood on my toes to pull boxes of photos from the high shelves. Some prints were placed neatly inside albums, others stacked on top of one another in small piles. Flipping through the perforated-edged photographs, I studied my grandparents at dinner parties, on holidays, at the ocean.

Nanu dressed in snorkeling gear on a boat over-looking the Gulf's waters. Nanu sitting on a train in Tokyo with a small Japanese girl on his lap. Him tickling her, and her mouth open wide with laughter. My grandmother, Nana, standing between Lisa and me, bald from brain surgery, her hands clutching our waists. Lisa and I leaned our heads toward hers and smiled.

I turned the laminated page. My Nana hugging Dicky from behind. She looked into the camera, her large white teeth exposed. Her hand held his bearded cheek, pinching it. My mother told me that when she and my father first started dating in their early twenties, Dicky was living in my grandparents' base-ment. She remembers the Drug Enforcement Agency raiding the place, recovering scales and pounds of marijuana. Dicky was eighteen when the armed, uniformed men entered my grandparents' house and flipped couch cushions upside down, pried under-neath carpets, took him out of there in handcuffs.

Another picture: Dicky sitting at a round dinner table wearing a pale pink shirt and tie, grinning directly at the camera. Next to him, my Nanu's eyes flashing across the scene. He looked confused, or unsure, his expression caught between nervous laughter and questioning. My Nanu spent years bailing Dicky out of trouble until one day, he stopped. One of the last times Dicky was arrested, and a family friend called to tell him, Nanu's response was, "I'm on the golf course. Let him sit there."

I turned the pages and uncovered moments. I wondered if one day someone would scan the pages of my life this way, uncovering my mistakes. I wondered

if I would be remembered by my own destruction—
my crawling on the floor face down against the
carpet, trying to breathe in a spilled powder. If I'd
be photographed like Dicky, and remembered as the
girl addicted to trouble—the girl who only felt normal
when hanging from the edges of things. That my way
of letting go had been by anesthetizing myself—that
I'd run off to the California mountains and physically
cut myself off from getting high, but thought about it
the entire time.

Krista paced into the room. She crouched down
and looked under the beds. "I know that palm tree
painting is here somewhere. He kept saying it was
almost finished, and it's not with any of the others."

I plucked a wallet-sized picture tucked behind the
corner flap on the inside cover of the album. Nanu in
the middle of my sisters and me, his hands clasped
around the front of my belly. My face scrunched up,
my eyes squinting, my chubby cheeks ballooned. He
looked down at me through square-framed bifocals. I
was three years old.

I placed the pictures in a neat stack and left them
on the carpet. I went out to the living room and took
a clock down from the wall. Black streaks ran across
its smooth cherry wood, its gold numbers prominent.
The clock had been part of the décor for as long as I
remembered, since my first memories of Nanu, in the
red ranch house in Massachusetts.

Krista followed me to the living room. "What are
you doing, taking everything, Gina?" She was half
teasing, half concerned. I wandered from room to
room trying to recollect, attempting to savor the
memories, but I only felt numb, the way one feels

after inhaling plates of food—consuming too much in order to distract herself. The numbness was mixed with an urgency to finish collecting—there would be no other time, no other chance, and these moments would pass, falling away like everything else.

We were confusing loss with belongings. Or, at least I was. I was still trying to discover where I belonged. I wanted to go back to the place I could not let go of; I wanted to go back to John. I'd left even though we weren't finished. I'd left when we were still at that stage of getting to know one another—of bonding through the telling of secrets, and holding others back. Denying it would be like cutting off a bloom just as it flourished, knowing it would only grow stronger—that you'd be back to tend to it.

I treaded around the house and gathered Nanu's things as if this would make him manifest, as if I would see him more clearly if I kept shoving t-shirts and books into my backpack. I picked up plastic cups lying on their sides and dumped out the balls he used for putting practice. My father hurried through the living room with a steel blade shovel. "What are you doing?" I asked.

"I'm going to dig up Nana and Uncle Dicky's ashes so you girls can drive them north. They're buried in the backyard. I need to find them before you leave. I made Nanu draw me a map of exactly where they were when he was in the hospital."

"You did?" I looked outside at the square patch of lawn. "Isn't it raining?" The sky darkened, and clouds gathered above the small house, above the abandoned clothesline that I used to hang onto and spin round as a girl. Raindrops tapped on the sills and screens, growing louder and harsher.

"It doesn't matter. I need to find them ASAP." Redness tinted his eyes. The bald spot on his head shone larger than I remembered it. My father trudged out the door. I watched him through the window, as the rain pasted his hair to his head.

*

I questioned the extent of what we would do to hold on to a beloved. Digging up the ashes at this exact moment was not going to save my father from having lost the man who raised him. Or his brother. I didn't know, still don't know, what it was like for my father growing up, since he had only mentioned his childhood while married to Brenda. Then, he spoke about how his father couldn't communicate with him and how his mother babied Dicky, but it was difficult to tell what the truth was—when he was with Brenda, no reliable form of truth existed.

"Hey, there's another painting in here, in the closet." Dawne called to Krista and me from the first bedroom off the hallway—our bedroom. Krista and I looked at one another. "Should I bring it out?"

"No, that's okay, we'll be right there." Krista rushed into the room, past the queen-sized bed we shared during our visits. And there it was. A replica of the award-winning palm tree painting, leaning up against the wall of the closet.

"Do you think it's finished? It looks just like the other one," I said. On the canvas, pink and yellow shades accented the dim clouds.

"He finished it," Krista said. "It only needs a frame."

I glanced at the desktop computer in the corner of the bedroom, by the dresser. Nanu used it often, making us cards for birthdays, graduations, and holidays. The last homemade card I received from him was for my college graduation the year before. The front had a cheerleader, mid-split, holding pom poms straight up in the air. The words WAY TO GO were typed on the front. Inside, it said, I AM SO PROUD OF YOU. I KNEW YOU COULD DO IT. NOW, ON TO THE NEXT CHAPTER. . . He printed a colored picture of a cartoon figure wearing a cap and gown next to the message.

Through the window, I saw my father outside shoveling. He was in a hurry, banging the dirt with the metal, sorting through the soil, digging. I felt sorry for him then, his hair soaked, as he attempted to uncover buried urns from a vague hand-drawn map on a flimsy piece of paper. He steadied his flashlight on the ground and kept digging, but I couldn't tell if he'd uncovered anything.

Krista looked at me. "What do you think, G? Time to go?"

My father, drenched, squeaked through the kitchen door, placing the two urns on the table for us. His shirt stuck to him, his sneakers sopping. "I found them," he said. I can't imagine what he felt; I don't know what his mother and brother meant to him. His father. This was the first I'd seen of his desperation, of this intense kind of love—real love. Although our situations differed, I understood my father's frantic need for this familiar contact, just as I understood my own.

I knew that if I returned to New Hampshire, to John, that it would not mend me—just as this digging, this urgency, would not make my father feel whole. I knew that if I returned, it would be for a man who did not have the capacity to love me back, a man who had a truer love to which I'd always come second. I knew that if I returned, I'd be going back to a man with whom I could not deny the sense of home I felt.

"You girls don't mind driving the urns up north? I'd rather not fly with them. I don't want anything to happen to them." I didn't know if I'd ever seen my father holding anything this dear to him.

"Joe, why don't I get you some dry clothes," Dawne said. "You're dripping everywhere. You must be cold."

After my father changed, he and Dawne helped us cover the paintings with trash bags and carry them out to the back of the truck. "Are you girls sure you don't want to stay the night and leave early tomorrow instead?"

Yes, we were sure. It was ten o'clock. I tucked the urns into a duffel bag in back, and my father helped me keep them upright as we positioned them in between suitcases. We said goodbye, and Krista slid into the driver's seat. I sat next to her and opened the atlas. She drove alongside the canal in the dark, rain splashing across the windshield. I took one last look at the park, the small hurricane-proof houses lined up like Monopoly houses waiting to be bought or sold or lost. I studied their colors, knowing it was unlikely we'd ever be here again. The wipers were frantic as we passed the pool, the clubhouse, the alligators. We drove out to the main road and headed to the interstate, northbound.

INDULGENCE

I'd been back in New Hampshire for over a month when John decided to quit heroin again. He'd been trying to quit all summer while I was in California, but he'd been unsuccessful. He told me he had not been able to find a fix, so he interpreted this as yet another sign. It was an exceptionally hot day for early October.

While I was away, John had finally moved out of his ex-girlfriend's place. Since his belongings were at Jacob's grandparents' house, and mine were in the cab of my truck, we bounced from one apartment to the next, crashing on friends' living room floors. That week, our friend, Marie, offered us her vacant apartment. She had moved across town, but her name was still on the lease for a few more days. *While you find a place*, she said.

The entire house was divided into four apartments. Marie's was on the far left, and the driveway was behind the house. Inside, we brought a hiking backpack filled with necessities: clothes, toiletries, a boombox, cigarettes, and a trash bag. The apartment had two floors, but we congregated on the first, using only the bathroom, one bedroom, the living room, and the kitchen that separated them. We claimed the bedroom in the back corner of the apartment, the room with the only shaded window.

The walls were white. The tile floors had been scrubbed clean with bleach. No furniture remained. In order to be filled with spirit, feng shui theory says one needs to be empty of worldly things. The color white, I remembered, is associated with purity. White is letting go. Surrendering.

I had hope.

We stocked the refrigerator shelves with tomato sauce and cheap champagne. We spread my insulated sleeping bag on the floor of the bedroom. While Jacob was at school, we made love on top of the sleeping bag. The boombox played Pearl Jam's song, "Indifference," the music soft and slow. I was on top of John, my knees pressed against the carpet. The twine chafed my skin. A small portable fan hummed as my flesh peeled, but I didn't mind the burning. My body fit his, like when I lay on the beach, and warm sand filled the folds of my skin. He swam inside of me while I climaxed. Orgasm was the single consistency of our relationship. Sex was the way we finished one another's sentences.

Afterward, John filled the ashtray with cigarettes while I filled my journal with words. Still naked, I sat up against the wall and began to shape a poem. He tucked his feet in between my crossed legs. Damp with sweat, I was content in this empty space. We had a place to sleep tonight, and perhaps John would have enough determination to beat his demon. Our conversation would percolate throughout the rooms. He would tell me about his fear, about feeling worthless when he wasn't high, and I would tell him about mine.

"Are you hungry?" he asked.

I nodded. This gesture was a lie. I wasn't hungry, but I aimed to distract him from the drugs.

John got up and went into the kitchen. "Is pasta okay?" he asked. "I didn't have enough money for anything else."

"Sure. It's fine."

"Are your knees okay?" He set the pot of water on the heating stove. My knees were red patches of raw, torn skin. I pulled my long, flowered skirt over my hips.

"Yeah, they will be." I laughed, and stretched a tank top over my head.

A few minutes later, John came back and positioned the boombox between us, a tabletop platform for the aluminum pot.

"Here," he said. "I think it's done." He brought a noodle to his mouth to test it. "Yup." He dumped the jarred sauce into the pot, and stirred it. "We only have one fork." He placed it in my hand.

John wore baggy jeans and a t-shirt that hung over his thin frame. His face was sparsely freckled, the outside of his gray eyes indented with wrinkles. His smile was a kind smile, usually forming at the end of a joke, and always accentuating his tough, worn skin. His hair was not short or long, but curled at the ends. When he spoke to me, he leaned in close. "Thank you," he said. He touched his lips to my ear. "For always sticking by me."

"Of course," I said.

I took a bite and handed the fork back.

*

After Nanu died, while I was staying back on Birch Street with my friends before driving out to

California, John stopped by to see me often. I had been attracted to him for the full year we worked together at the restaurant, while he sautéed gourmet dishes and I served them. The first time we spoke in the kitchen, he asked me where I was from. Our conversation grew intimate, as if we'd known each other for quite some time, and I attributed it to the fact that in a sense, we had. He stared straight into my eyes. I admired this trait. I tended to avoid eyes.

One of these nights, I didn't hear him come into the house, or up the stairs to my bedroom. The door cracked open, and I saw his silhouette. "Gina." He whispered in the dark, and shut my door behind him. The floor creaked in the old house with the rickety doorknobs.

"Yeah, hey," I said. "What are you doing?" The clock blinked 2 a.m. "What time is it really?" I asked.

"It's around 2:30," he said. "You said you'd be here." He sat on the edge of my bed and leaned down to kiss my cheek.

"Hey," I said again. I clutched his forearm.

"Is it okay that I'm here? Do you mind?"

"No, it's fine. I'm glad," I said. "How did you get here?"

"I walked." John's voice was slow and soft. I leaned over and grabbed a box of matches from the window-sill. I struck one, and lit three candles on the night-stand.

"I missed you," he said. His words were drawn out, the word *you* long and lingering. John climbed into the bed, a friend's old twin mattress left in the house before I had moved in. He leaned his head into the curve of my neck. He reached his hand up my shirt and traced my nipple. I felt it harden against his fingertips.

"What have you been doing? Where have you been tonight?" I asked.

"Hannah and I went down to Boston. Then, we started arguing. We argued the whole way home. And then back at the apartment, we argued more. I had to get out of there."

Hannah was John's ex-girlfriend of a few years, and he and Jacob still lived with her. Jacob's mother had left just after he was born, and Hannah treated him as her own.

"Arguing about what?" I asked.

"About everything. Which way to drive home. Everything. Just like our entire relationship, one long train wreck," he said.

In bed with John, I noticed his pupils in the candle-light. Dark and pin-sized. He scratched his neck and shoulders. Then his back. He lay on my bed with his head propped up against the pillow. He kept nodding down toward his chest, his eyes fluttering. Purple veins showed through his eyelids.

"I told Hannah I'm driving out to California with you," he said.

"You did?"

"Yep. I told her you're moving there, and that you need someone to help with the driving."

"What did she say?" I asked.

"She said okay."

"That's it?"

"That's it, just okay."

"What about Jacob? You'll be gone an entire week." I thought of Jacob's wide grin, his missing front tooth. The way he ran into the back door of the restaurant, and John lifted him into a bear hug, then spun him around.

"I'll ask his grandparents to take care of him."

Jacob. The letters of his tattoo were black and rounded, uncial script, but coiling up on the ends. I traced it with my thumb.

John didn't slur, but instead his voice droned, making a raspy humming sound, like a Tibetan throat singer. "I love being with you," he said. He consistently offered this tidbit. "You are such a good person. A smart person. You know what you want, and you take control."

I remained indifferent to these compliments. I did not view myself as good, or smart. As much as I fought it, my father and Brenda still drowned out any semblance of praise offered to me. I still heard their words, believed their meanings, their ruthless tones engraved, embedded in the deepest parts of me. But when John said these things, one part rang true: I knew what I wanted. Him. But, no, I did not control this desire. It controlled me. My emotions enslaved my rational mind. I knew I would go to California. But, on some level, I also knew I'd be back.

John said, "I want to do bad things to you." He lifted my shirt and slid his tongue along my skin. I teetered on the flimsy bridge between guilt and thrill. My guilt derived from failing to refuse him because of his habit. And also from ignoring that he still lived with Hannah, and his son, who needed his full attention. I was terrified of becoming even the slightest bit like my father, a person to whom infidelity came naturally, or like Brenda, a woman who would pull a father from his child.

But I succumbed to the thrill. I had a tendency

to sacrifice self-control for temporary gratification. It was comparable to the path John trekked if and when he found a fix. He knew that he was likely to be hurting himself, but he had to inquire anyway. He dove in.

I plunged. I wanted to know about his life. I wished to know why he felt the inexorable need to escape it.

When a person does heroin, the brain releases dopamine, a chemical responsible for the surges of euphoria. I once read that dopamine further drives addiction. It causes those who indulge to pursue pleasure at all costs, to love harder, to yearn intensely. I understood the way want only elicited more want. I was familiar with the mindset of addiction, the feeling that a crucial element is missing from one's life. I had been searching for it for as long as I remembered. I had been molded by my father and Brenda's expectations, any semblance of self I'd contained swallowed up, my senses dulled and deadened by their words and actions. I'd become vacant. So I'd turned to substances—cocaine and methamphetamines—inhaling anything I could get my hands on. I'd always sensed a void, and in turn, attempted to fill it.

*

John and I made love that night, and afterward, he said, "Tell me more about your Nanu. I wish I could have met him." Despite his altered state, John focused on my words. He watched my lips move, mesmerized. He listened. By candlelight, red patches blotched his face. He looked into my eyes but through them at the same time, as if he were a small child staring out a window watching snow fall. My fingers grazed his palms. His knuckles and fingernails were bitten down but evenly manicured. His flesh heated my forearms.

To me, John didn't look like he was in the "euphoric state" that heroin users describe. Instead, his mouth curled into a frown. His eyes drooped. He resided somewhere between falling asleep and waking up. It seemed that his body might jolt with sudden surprise at my voice, or a shadow, but it didn't.

John explained his and Hannah's situation like this: "We have a drug bond."

"What do you mean?"

"Heroin. We do heroin together."

I didn't feel surprise when John stated this. I hadn't consciously speculated about whether he was an addict; I'd already known, but like finding a lump on my breast and ignoring the doctor, I'd been unwilling to ask.

I knew then that he didn't love himself. We held this in common.

I saw all of his dimensions, and it was impossible to picture one without another. He was my friend in the kitchen who, when I spilled a few drops of milk, hurried over with a rag to wipe the floor, and said, "Don't worry Gina. I'll pick up your pieces." He was the hardworking cook who pulled double-shifts, his hands moving from pans to tongs to fryer, his neck glistening with perspiration, who, on his days off, carried his son in his arms when he stopped into the restaurant to pick up his paycheck. He was the patient single father who crouched down to help Jacob with his shoelaces, showing him how to tie them again and again, no matter how many tries it took.

He continued. "We don't shoot heroin. We snort it."

I found it fascinating that users were inclined to emphasize this fact. *I only snort it. I would never shoot it. I'm afraid of needles.* They seemed to believe that no one would die from snorting heroin, even when mixing it with other drugs. *Only shooters die.* These statements seemed to be accompanied by a certainty that their veins would not collapse, that they would not lead dysfunctional lives. No track marks, no problem.

"The first time we met she asked if I could get her some heroin. I said, 'yes.' I'd been doing it for a few years by then. And that's what started our relationship. Our common interest. After a few weeks, I moved into her place. The end."

*

That night in my bedroom, I understood John was high even before he told me about his habit, not because he hadn't offered a reason for the hour trip to Boston, not because one of our co-workers said that he used to do heroin and then "quit," and not because of his slurred voice and constant scratching, but mostly because of my uncle. From him, I recognized the pin-sized pupils. Of course, he was a shooter. He died.

John stayed until the six o'clock a.m. train sounded outside my bedroom window. He said, "I have to go. I feel guilty, still living with her and everything." He pronounced his guilt while coming down. The dopamine void. "I really need to get my own place," he said.

Outside the window, the sky was becoming brighter.

I looked around the room at the overflowing ashtray, the worn wicks of the candles, the hardened wax stuck to the end table, and assessed my nakedness. The scent of salt and sage. The radio still playing on low. I felt guilty too. But not to the point of regret. I saw no point in regretting an attraction I felt was beyond my control. I believed in the search for the missing element.

I closed my eyes as he sat up. I squished the pillow we had shared up against my cheek. It smelled like Polo cologne. I lay under the covers with only his TOOL t-shirt on. He leaned down and kissed my lips, then my cheek, up near my ear. "Sweet dreams, hon." He left wearing a black hooded sweatshirt. I dozed off under the bedspread while daylight crept in through the window.

*

In the white apartment, we sat next to one another on the island in the kitchen. John lit a cigarette. "Should I have Jacob stay with us tonight?"

"Won't he be scared?" I asked. "In a strange place with no electricity?"

"With me he's always moving around," he said. I looked down at the wounds on my kneecaps. I was aware of this life. I was living it with him. "But, yeah, no lights, you're right. I forgot about that," he said. He puffed on his cigarette with one hand, and gnawed his fingernails on the other. His eyes were turned down, thinking about one love only.

I went out to my truck and grabbed my camping flashlight and a bunch of fat candles that I'd tied together with string. There were two cars in front of mine in the driveway, belonging to people I hadn't yet seen. I wondered if they were curious about the young couple staying in the empty apartment with no electricity and no furniture.

I recalled one day, when John asked, "You know what heroin feels like?"

"What?" I asked.

"When you're high on heroin, your mother could be in the next room dying and you wouldn't even care. Even if she had been the best mother in the world. Nothing matters."

If this was what the elevation was like, then the coming off heroin must be like seeing your mother jump from a twenty-story building. Each moment starting to matter.

When I walked back into the apartment, John was on his cell phone in what should have been the living room, which faced the street in front of the house. Holes dotted the white paint, where pictures once hung. I spread the candles throughout the apartment. I placed one on a step stool in the bathroom, another on the boombox in the bedroom, and a couple throughout the kitchen. The echo of his voice bounced off the walls and ceiling. "Still no? Oh. Okay then. I'll try back later." He was looking out the window. I gathered that he had abandoned his decision to quit. I was accustomed to this fluctuation. I justified it because his relationship with heroin was not recreational. His body had woven it into its chemistry; it had made this sustenance a part of him.

The next night John and I lay together in our shared sleeping bag, but he kept turning over, flipping his limbs this way and that. "Oh," he said.

"Ohhh." His voice was high pitched, a wounded animal whimpering in the woods. The candles flickered. The vanilla scent mixed with cigarette smoke. His restless shadow reflected on the white ceiling.

"What is it?" I asked. "What's wrong?"

"It's starting to hurt," he said.

"What hurts?" I asked.

"I just hurt all over." He bent his knees and sat up, hugging them close. "My legs are cramping up." Beads of sweat glistened in blotches on his forehead. I looked at his half of the pillow, the cotton stained with perspiration.

"How long have you been sweating like this?" I asked.

"I don't know. A little while. Since we laid down, I guess." He was rocking back and forth. "I feel like I might throw up." He put his forehead down and cradled it in his hands. "I don't know what to do here, Gina. I don't know if I can do this." He straightened his legs and stretched them out in front of him, wiggling his toes.

"Of course you can do this. I'm here with you," I said.

John had attempted to abstain before, but had never reached the point of physical sickness. He had always found a fix.

On the floor, in this emptiness, John detoxed. He hollowed out. His hair soaked his scalp with sweat. I felt like we were hitting a wall, each coming at it from the opposite side. Both tired from pushing. "I'm scared," he said. "I'm not sure what's happening to me." He brushed my hand away from his shoulder. "It hurts," he said again.

He was giving up, and I was the eternal cheer-leader. I was trying to convince him that it was okay—okay that his mother was dying, that his world collapsed—it was okay to care. To feel anguish from all moments mattering at once. I insisted that my capacity to love him could exceed his need, but I also knew this might be a delusion.

I thought about my uncle, found dead in a warehouse parking lot, his arms scarred with track marks. He was found hunched over the steering wheel in his truck, a used needle on the passenger floor. My uncle lay in an open casket, his skin pasty, his beard intact, his face an orange hue. In the weeks before he died, he gave my sisters and me boxes of jewelry and watches, perfume left at his apartment by old girlfriends and friends, as if he was taking inventory of his belongings. At the funeral, his longtime girlfriend, Nikki, stood over his coffin crying, and told my mother and sister, "If I hadn't left him, I'd be in this coffin with him."

With heroin addicts, the brain cells that produce dopamine eventually shut down, and they permanently lose their ability to produce it at all. This happens as a result of years of depletion. We do not have an endless supply; it becomes used up. I speculated the chances of John's cells surrendering. I wondered if he would be able to experience serenity again, or ever. I wondered if he would be filled, or if I would. Would he consider his life devoid of meaning without drugs? Would I ever fill this space? He indulged heavily. His addiction was fierce. It came before me, and it came before his son.

John was sniffling now. He lay in the fetal position.

His arms and legs twitched, making rapid kicking movements. "I'm just so tired of all this. I don't want to include you in this misery. You know that, right?"

*

I was already an integral part of John's world. He woke each morning needing a fix. Without an alarm clock, he jumped up, startling me. "I have to go," he said. And I'd know his mission had begun.

But I could not remove myself. I experienced surges of bliss when we were together, and then, when he did not meet me at a given time, or keep his word, they were followed by dismantling disappointment. I became elevated by this man, with whom I took walks in the rain in the middle of the night, him always clasping my hand. With whom I could talk about my father's rage, about his abandoning me, and who listened when I admitted that I believed I feared death because I was murdered in my past life. With whom I lay in bed for days, trading meals and showers for flesh. And then, when he said he'd be back in a half hour and instead disappeared for days at a time to look for a fix, I worked long days and tried to forget him, to tell myself I could not deal with this—I had to leave him. But I didn't.

"I'm a bad father. A bad boyfriend. A bad friend." Tears dripped down his nose.

"Don't say those things. You are a great father." I believed this. I believed this because when I allowed Jacob to try on my skirts and dresses, John said, "He's just expressing himself." I believed this because when we went for a drive, he pulled his son onto his lap and sang him the Led Zeppelin song, "All of My

Love." I believed this because, when it came to my own father, I had only a few decent memories interspersed in an otherwise colorless world, so unlike the vibrant, tender moments John and Jacob shared.

"I'll get you something to drink," I said. I grabbed a bottle of Merlot from the kitchen, and uncorked it.

I handed him the bottle. He chugged it, swallowing more than half the bottle in one gulp.

"Feel better?" I asked.

He gave a slight nod. "My stomach really hurts though." Goose bumps popped up on his arms, hairs standing up around them. I felt his forehead. Cold and clammy.

I once read a recovered addict's story, in which she said that all the bad points of heroin still don't add up to that one perfect moment: that moment heroin addicts live for. Her words reminded me of my addiction to him. Instead of his failure to show up for certain events, I focused on our dinners, him grilling yellowfin tuna garnished with asparagus, and pulling chairs over for Jacob and me while he sat on a garbage can. I listened to his epiphanies: "I know I need to get sober, for you and for my son. I know I can do it. It will be okay." I replaced the painful moments like burnt out candles—by tossing them out and seeking a new fresh scent.

"Gina, get some sleep. You have to work in the morning. I'll be all right. Go ahead, doze off. I might have to be in the bathroom for a while."

It was difficult for me to think about sleep, although I was exhausted. I thought about John being sober—the image of his mother, killed by a drunk driver when he was four—dying in the next room. It mattered, and it wouldn't stop. He could not do anything to prevent it. Who wouldn't give in to the fix, the only thing to cease the agony? I buried my head in the damp pillow.

*

Minutes later, I was dreaming. Nanu was there, and he asked me to help him cool his skin. Blisters from burns covered his arms. He pointed to glass mugs filled with water, overflowing with ice cubes. We were in front of an enormous mirror, and I was standing behind him. "Help me pour it over the burns, GG." I grabbed the glasses and started pouring, trying to cool his lesions. I was hasty, splashing the water, trying to relieve him. When I looked back up at the mirror, it was no longer my Nanu, but my uncle, and the burns were boils from shooting heroin. He smiled with his mouth closed. The two people meshed into one, and in the dream, I was not sure which one I missed more, or if it was both.

My Nanu couldn't bear trying to help his son any longer, only to be disappointed. At my uncle's funeral, he wailed and said, "What a waste." I imagined that he felt the wounds as his own. I imagined he spent his life trying to find relief.

With John, I'd learned that heroin causes skin infections or boils.

And that when addictions are fulfilled, endorphins are released. Endorphins serve as a pain reliever.

John was in severe pain now. He picked up his cell phone.

"What are you doing?" I asked.

"I have to get a ride into the city, Gina. I'm really

hurting." He spoke into the phone. "Um, yes, I'm calling about the train schedule. What time does the train go into the city in the morning?" It was three a.m. "Shit," he said, and ended the phone call.

"I don't want you to go down there," I said.

"I can't get there any time soon anyway. The train doesn't go until tomorrow afternoon."

John didn't have a car. I lit a cigarette and took a swig from the wine bottle. I put my head in my hands. "Let's just get through the night. I can give you a ride when it's daylight." I mumbled this.

"I thought you had to work," he said.

"I do, but I'll figure it out. I'll make something up."

*

When you are in love with a drug addict, you learn to lie, just as they do. When someone notices that he is obliterated, you blame it on him having a few too many drinks. When he loses his job, you pretend that he quit to find a better one. When he doesn't have transportation, you blame it on the fact that he is supporting a child, not a habit. Slowly, addiction changes you as well. You don't believe the words you utter, and you no longer believe your own judgment.

*

The pink hues of dawn lightened the shade covering the bedroom window. I had dozed off again, and when I woke up John's head was at my feet. His hands were wrapped around my calves, his legs scrunched up to his chest. He was shaking again. "Come on, let's go," I said. It was six a.m.

"Okay." He jumped up. "Thank you."

We headed down the highway, my eyes on the road, while John tried to relax in the passenger seat. "I'm sorry," he said. "That you had to give me a ride."

"It's okay." I could no longer stand watching his hands twitch, his legs tremble.

By the time I dropped him off and returned to town, I realized that I was an hour late for work. I called to tell my boss I had car trouble. "I'll be there as soon as I can," I said.

On my way, Marie called and asked if we could get our belongings out of the apartment. *To make space for the new tenants*, she said.

"No problem," I told her. "As soon as I get out of work."

I hung up and called John. "It's time for us to get out of there," I said.

"It is? Don't worry. We'll find something. We always do."

When I got to the restaurant, my co-worker, Jill was working the breakfast function. "Is everything okay, Gina?"

"Yeah, I'm fine. Hey, I was wondering, do you think John and I can stay at your place tonight?" I asked.

"Yeah, sure. Are you sure you're okay?" she asked.

"Yeah. We just still haven't found a place," I said. "Thanks." I grabbed a pot of coffee, and brought it over to the table to refill the mugs.

Jill followed me. She placed scrambled eggs in front of the patrons, but she was still looking at me, searching for a telling expression.

After work, I went back to the apartment to pack up, which only took a few minutes. I held the boombox in one hand, a duffel in the other, and I wore the backpack. On my way out, before closing the door, I took one last peek around to make sure we had left no trace. The apartment looked brighter without our scattered possessions. White and inviting.

SHADOWS ON
THE SIDEWALKS

In late November, John decided to check himself into rehab. It had been almost two months since we stopped bouncing around from apartment to apartment, crashing on floors and couches—two months since I'd used the money I saved from working at the restaurant to rent a one bedroom on Middle Street. We had shelter, a space to put our sparse belongings, mostly clothes and books and music. I found a used loveseat on the side of the road, and a friend gave us a kitchen table. I picked up my hibiscus and rubber trees from my old place on Birch Street, and we blew up an air mattress to use as a bed.

John brought kitchen supplies from the restaurant where we worked—tongs and spatulas and sheet pans. We made a corner for Jacob's toys, even though his primary residence was at his grandparents' house. Piles of his videos and books and model helicopters were strewn about the apartment. On the evenings we weren't working, John made dinner while Jacob and I sat on the living room's hardwood floor and finished his kindergarten homework. We traced shapes and colored ice cream cones, and I covered his small hand with mine, helping to guide it, as he pressed rainbows of color into paper. After dinner, Jacob went home to his grandparents' house. John and I made love, and then lay together, my head molded into his neck, my hand on his chest, his fingers interlacing mine while we watched movies on VHS on the old television set. We listened to music, made love again, talked by candlelight, the inside of our thighs pressed against one another. When John checked himself into rehab, we were finally making a home.

The day John left, we took Jacob to the playground. I sat on the curb and waited while they talked alone by the swing set. John pushed Jacob. His feet dangled as he swung. Deep orange leaves fell from a nearby oak. I took a drag off my cigarette, smoke swirling up into the chilly air, and ruminated about how John dressed his son like himself. Jacob wore diminutive, tan cargo pants and an Adidas visor. He had the same dirty blond hair, cut short, but longer on top. They looked like a set of twins, except years apart.

I considered Jacob's tough little life, how his mom had deserted him, his bouncing back and forth between his grandparents' house and mine, and the bond he formed with Hannah, who was still a part of his life, but with whom he no longer lived. I wanted to help look out for Jacob, to be another person he could depend on, but I didn't want to become part of a pattern. I didn't want to be a woman who tore through his life without thinking, or who pretended to be someone she was not. John was the first single father I'd known. I was used to the idea of fathers leaving, but when a mother was absent, it stood out, seemed like the child hovered over a black hole, trying not to fall in.

When they walked toward me, to our parking spot, Jacob's cheeks were shining with tears. John grimaced, shaking his head. His hair hid part of his gray eyes, and his face looked weathered, defeated. I knew he had his mind made up about leaving, and I was glad, although I hated to see him go.

We climbed into my truck, Jacob squeezing between us, and I fastened his seatbelt. I turned up the heat. Snuggling his head against my ribs, he said, "My Daddy's sick. He's going to the hospital for a while."

"I know, honey." My eyes watered and I swallowed hard as I started the truck. "He'll be okay, though. He'll be back soon. Before you even know it." My voice cracked at the end of the sentence, as if I was about to lose it. As if no words, no matter how important, could bring it back.

John spread his hand over his son's knee. He rolled the window down a crack, and I caught a glimpse of the tattoo on the inside of his forearm, the one I traced with my eyes on the day we met. The radio echoed Led Zeppelin's "All of My Love," and John began to sing. He unfastened Jacob's seatbelt, pulling him onto his lap, his mouth to his son's ear while he hugged him tight against his chest. He lifted Jacob's legs horizontally, and cradled his short body lengthwise, bouncing him in his arms. Jacob giggled, not the way he usually did when his father did this, but more intermittently, happy to be held.

John stilled him, and Jacob said, "I don't want you to go to the hospital, Daddy."

"Don't worry, hon, I'll be back soon." He flipped Jacob back to a vertical position, back in the space between us, keeping an arm wrapped around his body. He kissed his son's head just above his right ear. "You and me, we're together for life—we have all kinds of time together." It is the type of statement parents make to their children and mean, clinging to their words while searching for normalcy, for predictability. It is the type of statement parents depend on when they have nothing else to hold on to.

*

When John and I met, I felt I'd heard hints of his voice before, seen glints of his eyes, recognized his hands, how his fingers looked strong, his nails short and trimmed and clean. I'd seen the man who helped me find cocktail napkins and croutons in the basement filled with dry goods, the man who always offered to make a veggie stir-fry for me to take home during an afternoon lunch break. I'd seen the man who stopped by my house every few days, bringing a joint for us to smoke while we listened to 311 and talked about our pasts—he told me about his aunt, who he lived with when his mother was killed and his dad was in Vietnam, about his stepmother, who made him do chores while his father remained indifferent, about how he eventually dropped out of prep school, met Jacob's mother, ended up here, in this small New Hampshire town.

I'd seen the man who looked into my eyes whenever I spoke, who listened while I told him about my desire to travel westward, to see the largeness of the world, about how I could never seem to find a place that felt like home. I'd seen the man with whom I went for walks on sun-soaked days that New Englanders wait for all winter—with whom I barely noticed dusk approaching as we wandered into the depths of the night, the sky speckled with stars. Our friendship grew quickly and smoothly, like staring straight ahead in an airport and stepping onto one of those swift conveyor belts. By the time I found my footing, I stepped off, realizing I was where I needed to be.

Despite our efforts, heroin had become a third party in our relationship, not like John's son, but more like another woman I had accepted as ours. She was paused, suspended in the small space between us. She hovered over the mattress on which we slept. She waited for us when daylight broke. He tried to resist her, but he could not, and as any woman who'd trained herself to accept the unacceptable, I tried not to notice.

*

I drove John up to the twenty-eight day rehab following the Kancamagus Highway, New Hampshire's scenic road. We wove in between mountains and edged along rivers and streams, the auburn leaves bold against the sage-colored land. In the truck, John was silent.

I placed my arm on his, smoothing the veins with my fingers, squeezing his forearm muscle. "He'll be okay," I said. I knew he was thinking of Jacob. "You're a good father." I reflected on how happy Jacob always was to see John, how he'd run in and out of the restaurant's kitchen laughing and squealing, how John would tie a miniature kitchen apron around Jacob's waist so he could pretend to be a chef too. I noticed when he fixed Jacob a plate of green beans and corn, throwing some grilled chicken on the plate, insisting that he needed protein. I watched while he packed his son's duffel bag for an overnight at our house, placing Sponge Bob and tiny sneakers and hats neatly beside one another, and clipping Jacob's mittens to the zipper of his jacket.

When I'd said this before, that he was a good father, he thanked me, but today he said, "It isn't true. He needs more." We were stopped at a red light when he said this and he was tilting his head downward, looking at me sideways, his face guilty. "*You* need more."

My hand was holding the shifter firmly, and he covered it with his. He felt the tops of my fingers, my knuckles, caressed my wrist. "That's why I'm going."

The light turned green, and he moved his hand from mine, rested it on my thigh. I knew he was right about my needing more. I said nothing.

John and I had not made the life we'd convinced ourselves was possible when I had returned from California. My first night home, we stayed on a friend's couch, the air conditioner rattling in the window, the stereo on low. We made love with me sitting on top of him, one side of his face lit by candlelight, while the other remained dark. My breasts grazed against his chest, my hair fell forward onto his shoulders. We talked while he was inside of me, our shadows on the walls and ceiling showing two bodies blended or one larger figure, depending on the angle of flickering light.

"Things are so different now than before you left," he said.

"What do you mean?"

"I can focus on you now. On us. I don't live with her anymore. I don't have to feel guilty. I'm fully single." In the months before I left, I was the girl a few miles down the road who waited for John to visit when he wanted to escape his troubles. I was the girl who represented his fabricated life, the one without a girlfriend and a son. Even before we had been together in bed, I was infidelity. We were infidelity. It was there at the restaurant, in the steam rising off the plates he handed me. It was on the streets we walked, when our hands brushed near one another's, skimming and grazing, but never clasping. It was in our lengthy, contemplative stares. When John and Hannah broke up, he and Jacob were still living in her apartment for some time before I left for California. I had been glad to go because I'd grown tired of feeling like a mistress. I decided that I couldn't continue with a man slipping into my bedroom at two a.m., only to see him the next day with the woman he lived with—when I could still smell his cologne on my neck—having to say hello to him as though it was for the first time that day.

On top of him, naked, I rested my cheek on his exposed chest. I didn't ask about his and Hannah's final parting, or the moving out. I didn't ask if they were still in contact, and I didn't care. His peach soap scent mixed with my lilac shampoo and I breathed him in, breathed us in as if we were characters in a short-lived dream, as if it would be daybreak soon, and we'd have to wake up.

We moved to the floor and lay side by side on the carpet by the light of three candles. We flicked our cigarettes into the ashtray on the coffee table.

"I really want to be with you," he said.

I stared him straight in the eyes. His lashes quivered, and I saw his sadness. "Me too," I said. I rolled over onto my side and rested my ear on his warm chest. Groovechild's song, "Riverside," played softly.

"Sounds like you were pretty healthy out there in Cali," he said.

"Yeah, I was. But I was really lonely too."

*

Our relationship had always suited nighttime, its uncertainties, the hope huddled underneath the fear, the inspirations born of danger. I thought of what our nighttimes had become, how along with sex and talk and music, they now consisted of empty baggies with powder remnants, and hollowed out bottles. At night, we sat up in bed drinking wine and passing joints. John got up periodically to snort the powder trailing across the bureau.

One night, he knelt on my bedroom floor with a razor blade. A square hand mirror rested on the bedroom rug. He cut the powder and arranged it into short, crooked lines. "You have no interest in this?" he asked.

"No."

"Good."

"Do you sometimes wonder what it would be like if we did it together?" I asked. I thought of his drug-induced bond with Hannah. I thought about the drug bonds I'd formed with different men—the incessant talking—the comfort automatically found with the other who shares your plane of existence. How by wounding yourselves together you become inextricably connected, like twins who explain one sibling breaking an arm and the other rushing to the hospital in pain. How you can become parts of one another, with or without sex. Two people who will trade limbs and lives. Who will die for one another, and for their one love.

"No," he answered. "I would never want you to be part of my hell."

*

In the White Mountains, we stopped at a mom-and-pop pharmacy. We stalled there, circling around the store, peering through glass cases at watches and bracelets. When we did errands together, it was usually at the grocery store, shopping for egg noodles or chicken breasts for the three of us, but in this unique place with greeting cards and toiletries and pharmaceuticals, we sought the necessities for someone who was staying away from home, things to help the pain of detox subside.

I thought about how Jacob related rehab, where a person mends himself through abstinence, to a hospital, where he is hooked up to IVs, pumped with drugs to kill infection or disease, to speed up recovery. How rehab was almost the opposite of a conventional hospital, since John's medicine, the substance that prevented his body from illness, would be taken away. In rehab, John would be denied the exact thing his body hungered for in order to stay stable. I had no misconceptions about the strength of heroin, or the challenges of withdrawing from it. I realized that even if rehab worked, if he was able to get clean, the absence of this drug would be as prominent as its presence, like a woman he could now resist but could not forget.

We exited the store, John holding a plastic bag with the things I'd bought him: Advil, a new razor, and three dark chocolate bars.

Rehab was an old barn turned into a farmhouse. It had a sloped roof with black shingles, and a rustic wrap-around porch. The brown house was backed by snowcapped mountains, surrounded by open fields spotted with sugar maples and yellow birches. The air was colder here; I carried John's winter coat and hat. Inside the front door was a staircase leading up, a kitchen to the right, an office to the left. It smelled like brownies.

On our left, inside the office, was a brunette, smiling woman. "Hello, I'm Maggie. Come on in. Welcome." The room, with shelves of books and warm, hardwood walls and flooring, reminded me of the inside of a secluded Vermont cabin. Maggie sifted through the stacks of folders scattering her desk and said, "John?"

He nodded, looking down at the red shag rug. "We've been expecting you." I wondered how many people had entered this office, how many had stayed, or had left too early. I wondered how many had repossessed their lives, how many had not. He squeezed my hand as I studied Maggie's large earrings made of green sea glass. Hardcover books were stacked neatly on the desk: *You Are Not Alone*, *Addiction*, *Alcoholics Anonymous*. She handed John the guestbook.

"If you'll both sign in please." She looked at me. "It's just routine. Anyone who comes in needs to sign, even if you're not staying." Along the wall, shelves held binders labeled *Starting Over, Cleaning House, Life Skills.* Rehab is a place where addicts reconstruct their lives; they are taught how to maintain jobs, open bank accounts, budget their incomes. They develop short-term goals, create lists of things to do that don't mention going after a fix.

John had said to me, "You and my son are all I need to stay clean," and even though I knew this was not true, I clung to these moments of reprieve, his words swelling inside me like surges of hope.

I knew that the life John and I had built together was unlike most versions of "normal." Most people didn't live with little furniture and no savings; they didn't wake up craving a fix, or come home to an empty apartment when their lover had disappeared to go find one. But, at this point in my life, there was no one else who heard me the way John did, who could finish my sentences, who could speak to me through touch alone, who understood what I meant when I said nothing. I knew that most couples didn't go for walks in the middle of the night for no particular reason—that they didn't have trouble sleeping, so decide to venture out into erratic elements on foot, hand in hand, recapping their lives, as if by walking they were able to move away from them somehow, to leave behind the times before they were together.

John and I had trekked for miles and miles across the mill town where we lived, most of this ground covered within the stillness of night. There was something about our walking, our shadows on the sidewalks, our movement and motion, that deepened our understanding of one another; as if we both accepted the possibility that our lives were intersecting at this crucial point, but with no hope of the future, no promise of tomorrow. It was often during these walks, when the sun was down and as the world was sleeping, that we were able to discover the most about ourselves and one another, about how we fit. Perhaps he and I were willing to chance that we had nothing but the present; this is why we grasped so tightly to it—and to one another—knowing that at any moment, with the light of day, it could fall away.

*

John dropped my hand to take the pen from Maggie. She said, "I'll show you around." Maggie led us downstairs and we walked down a hallway lined with framed quotes: *God grant me the serenity* and *Take one day at a time.* At the end of the hallway was a cement room that resembled a half-finished basement; it was filled with furniture, but without a carpet or painted walls. It had televisions and a ping pong table and coffee pots, with different doors to meeting rooms. A cluster of tables and folding chairs filled one corner of the room. Maggie looked at me. "This is where you'll visit," she said. She showed us the smoking area, which was outside the sliding back doors of the basement.

She brought us up one flight and said to John, "I'll show you to your room next, so you can get settled in." She looked at me politely, and I knew that my part of the tour had ended. "You don't have a room-mate yet, but you will," she said. John nodded, indifferent. We both knew that his room would look like the kind in a dormitory. Two beds, a large window, a desk with a shelf, and closets with sliding wooden doors. This was not his first time in rehab, and this was not my first time visiting one.

"I'll let you two say goodbye," she said. "But please, make it quick—house rules."

I had a dreaded feeling, as if I was dropping him off in the woods in the middle of nowhere without food or a tent—without anything to fend off the wolves. I didn't want to imagine him in a room, on a sterile bed without me curled up next to him, without music or candlelight, without our skin touching. I didn't want to imagine him trying to sleep through the night sweats and nausea and muscle spasms we knew he would have. I didn't want to imagine the fear that would envelope him when he couldn't have a fix—the remembrance of the last time he saw his mother, of how she was there and then gone—his worry about Jacob and how he would endure his own mom's abandonment. I caught myself wondering how and if he would survive this breaking apart, this mending. I wondered how and if I would.

In the hallway, John leaned into me and touched my face. "Thank you," he said, and kissed my lips as I tried to still them. "I know this isn't easy. You've already done this—the halfway house thing. Waiting for someone. I have no right to ask you to do it again." He was referring to my previous relationship, with Corey, a man I'd spent two years loving while I was in college, despite his being in jail for drug charges. Whom I'd talked about with John in our early days of working together at the restaurant when he was still with Hannah, and we were just getting to know one another as friends, the two of us standing in the kitchen while he sliced peppers into smooth, delicate strips, and I polished forks and knives and spoons with a rag sprayed with Windex, the chemical smell stinging the inside of my nose. I'd grown up with Corey, so I had already loved him before we'd become romantically involved, but after he was sentenced, things intensified. We wrote pages upon pages of letters, I accepted collect phone calls even though I couldn't afford them, and I drove the meandering roads two hours each way to visit the prison each Sunday. And when our relationship failed to sustain itself after he was released, I was shattered, inconsolable, barely able to leave my house without smoking a joint, without creating a barrier of fog between me and the world. John knew all of this, just as he knew that I'd been torn apart by Nanu's death, that my father was still out of the picture, that abandonment was a recurring instance in my life. He knew that he was the only one who took me seriously when I broke, when my fear became so potent that I could not move.

He knew that I had come home for him.

"You're not asking me to do anything," I said. "This is what I want." John concentrated on my eyes, as if in search of his own reflection. He took my hands in his, studied my nails, then pulled me into his embrace.

When I returned to Maggie's office to sign out of the house, I was crying. Maggie asked me if I had someone I could talk to, if I had help for myself. "Yes," I said, without giving her question even a moment's thought. "Thank you."

*

When I returned home without John, the apartment was quiet and empty. My footsteps were loud against the floor, and I turned on the music, the volume on high. I surveyed the contents of the kitchen: the spider plant John's stepmom gave him hanging from the ceiling, our three seats surrounding the table in a semi-circle, John's CDs stacked on the island countertop in the kitchen. Above the stove was a brown vintage frame encompassing the macraméd words, *Having someplace to go is home, Having someone to love is family, Having both is a blessing.*

I wondered how I ended up here. I had rented this apartment with the two of us in mind. If not for John, perhaps I would've stayed west and started growing a garden of herbs, or driven the Alaskan highway until I reached the wilderness, or gone off to the Virgin Islands for the winter, as was tentatively planned. But once here, I'd become someone content with the thought of making Jacob's school lunches, of staying in one place, committed to a lease, paying the electric bill.

The truth was, I had no idea what I was doing with my life, with the college degree I hadn't even thought about using. I had wanted to be a writer since the third grade, but I was writing nothing more than entries in my journal, which I scribbled while drunk and distracted. I was stuck in the temporary world of restaurants—of quick, instant, fleeting money, of loud voices calling out orders and yelling for pick up, the blend of anger and laughter, of hot plates and blistered hands, where the group of us played pool and smoked pot in the back room of the upstairs bar after we locked the doors, where I dabbed aloe on John's hands and arms, bandaged them after he burned himself in the kitchen. I was consumed by a constant rush of adrenalin—a world that helped me forget and bury my chronic anxiety—the culmination of years of fear that I would never make it beyond my father's grips, the walls of his and Brenda's house.

When I left California, one of my roommates had sent me off with a tribal picture she'd drawn, pink and black ink streaking up and down the page. On the back of the picture, she'd written a long note, and the last line said, *You are a light shining to everyone but yourself.* I contemplated her words as I slunk back into the loveseat, remembering my relationship with Corey, a relationship defined by absence, teetering on the possibility of its potential, of what it might become if only the circumstances were not what they were. I remembered the way I exhausted myself by focusing so intensely on this impossible union. When my roommate gave me this letter, I thought, *But this is who I am. This is what I have to give.*

By the time I met John, I was overly familiar with emptiness. I had adapted to unpredictability, was used to disappointment, to clinging to small moments of respite among chaos. I don't know if I realized it then, but I was not so far from the girl who starved herself well into her teen years, or the girl who smiled when expected, no matter how distraught. I had once again become what was expected of me, except that now I expected it of myself; I would be the fixer, the savior, once again a ceramic figurine afraid of breaking.

In the empty apartment, the lights still off, I drew the shades. I turned off the music. I wanted nothing to remind me of John, although everything did, all our memories rushing at me as I sank into the loveseat. Most nights after work, I slouched into the mustard-colored Victorian couch in the corner of the restaurant's lounge and dozed off. When John finished in the kitchen, he always ran up the stairs looking for me, his steps loud, climbing two stairs at a time. I'd hear him say hello to my co-worker, Jill, as she washed the beer taps, his voice waking me. "Hey, babe." When he reached me, I opened my eyes, taking note of how the dim lighting reflected his hair's uneven ends in the window behind him. I loved his hair—how the straggled ends looked highlighted even though they weren't, and how the darker streaks blended into the lighter ones, curling to rest in creases of his neck. His lips pressed against mine, and I leaned into his kiss. He grabbed my hand and led me down the stairs, and we walked home.

Just yesterday morning, I heard John and Jacob's footsteps in the kitchen, Jacob's lighter and quicker, as he ran into the bedroom. "Hi, sweetie," I whispered, yawning, holding the covers up tight underneath my armpits.

"Hi, Gina." Jacob approached the side of my bed and squinted his green eyes, leaning his head to one side while he grinned. He handed me a red rose. "This is for you." The flower surpassed the length of his arm.

"Thank you." I touched the petals to my nose and breathed in. "It smells amazing." I smiled at John.

"I had nothing to do with it." He laughed. "Really, I didn't. It's his grandparents' anniversary. He saw the roses on their kitchen table and asked his grandmother if he could bring you one."

Jacob stood by my bed, eye level with me. "Do you like it, Gina?"

I was not a rose person—from John I would have expected yellow irises or calla lilies, or Gerber daisies, but seeing Jacob's face peering up at me, waiting for my response, I could imagine no better way to wake up. "I do," I said. "It's beautiful. Just like you." I tapped his round nose with the flower. "Now let's go put it in some water."

"Okay," he said, in his raspy, excited voice, and ran out of the bedroom. John took the rose from my hand, leaned down, stuck his head under the comforter and kissed my chest, his mouth making me pause. He kissed my neck, my skin tingling underneath his breath, and we rose up together and hugged, him still hanging on to the flower. While I dressed, John found a vase in the pantry, put the rose in water, rested it on the nightstand.

These are the times I chose to remember.

*

John ended up signing himself out of rehab after five days instead of twenty-eight, the duration it can take for physical withdrawal symptoms to diminish. He told me only a bit about it, like a man who had come back from war. He mentioned the delirium tremens and hallucinations he had in the dorm-like bedroom. "Ray was there," he said. Ray was the large, pale man with the booming voice who sold him dope in the city. "It was completely real. He was there in that room with me. And he had heroin." When John said this, I imagined his lack of dopamine, of pleasure, and the void it created—the hollowness. I imagined him looking for glimmers of light, hints of hope that were released when he got high, but finding none.

When John came back early, I didn't ask if Maggie tried to make him stay, or if the counselors encouraged him to try harder to recover, to leave twenty-three days later renewed. I knew that even if he had stayed for the duration there would still be a slim chance of him ever feeling renewed—he might always feel incomplete, a man tortured by the lover with whom he left too many things unfinished.

When John came home early, he said, "I have always been with an addict. But not you—you are a good woman." And I wondered if I was.

TOMORROW

O ne winter day, a couple of months after John left rehab, the three of us walked through town, Jacob's skin raw, his tiny hands red and swollen from the New England air. "Daddy, I'm freezing," he said, a small cry escaping.

"I know, hon, I know." John stopped and bent down so he was eye level with his son. He cupped his own hands around his nose and mouth, breathed into them, then fastened them around Jacob's. He rubbed his son's palms together to generate some kind of heat. Jacob's grandmother had forgotten to pack his mittens, and I knew John blamed her, but I also knew it might have been the result of a miscommunication, or the rushed exchange of the overnight bag, or an impulsive change in schedule due to his needing to find a fix.

The three of us walked. Our eyes focused on the road ahead. We wove down the streets of our broken-down-yet-up-and-coming mill town, a place that mixed transients and townies and college students. Past the hardware store, and the four-dollar movie theater, past the homeless woman pushing her shopping cart down the sidewalk. Our legs raced with the urge of the brisk, bitter season, of a gray, silent sky. Of snow about to fall.

John and I were in the business of moving. We

worked long days, him grilling steaks and sprin-
kling parmesan on pasta, me pouring beers and
mixing martinis, scampering up and down the stairs
carrying trays of food and empty, dirty plates. Hours
flew by when we didn't stop to eat, or break for the
bathroom, or even wipe sweat from our foreheads,
our lower backs. Other times, when the restaurant
was slow, we met in the basement, where empty
liquor bottles piled up behind the ice machine, and
the linen dryer hummed. We sank down into crev-
ices and corners, finding warmth in closeness, hiding
away like creatures who crawled into small spaces
searching for morsels of food. We were beyond
hungry. Underneath the weight of one another, our
bare bodies shed layers of who we had been, our
coming together a mutual understanding that the
only thing we had to hold onto was *now*. And then,
we did it all over again.

Jacob kept walking—we all did—crossing the
intersections and side streets, passing the concrete
building with the mural of trees and rivers, the
music store with guitars and drums displayed in
the window. John and I were on either side of Jacob,
clasping his hands. His palm was so small it felt fake
to me, its size a reminder of a doll I once owned, except
for the prominent blue veins, the pulse of blood. He
was quiet now, as if, at least for this moment, he had
accepted his fate. I missed his voice—its rasp and
pitch, its sweetness coating the knowledge of where
he might be if not here with us.

I grabbed onto Jacob tighter, holding the puffy
sleeve of his coat as we scrambled down icy sidewalks,
his cheeks splotched with red, his eyes watering. He

began to cry again, and I wanted to put him into a car, blast the heat, ask a driver to deliver us to a house where chicken soup was warming on the stove, hot chocolate steaming from a mug. A traditional house with two married parents and a dog scurrying from room to room, with enough food and clothes and lots of books. But we were headed somewhere else.

We had gone too far to turn back now. Walking was the way we traveled. We spent entire days trudging through snow, traipsing through pouring rain. We watched the ash trees and birches grow leaves that turned red and orange, pungent colors that exploded before departing, their skeletal branches patched with snow. We roamed underneath the sweltering heat of the sun. In motion, we remade ourselves, distracted by the notion of having to be everywhere and nowhere at once. In constant flux, we dared to forget the main mission—John's seeking out a substance, *the* substance, that made him whole, a powder that had changed the chemistry of his brain.

When John was not around, I walked Jacob to the store and bought cigarettes while he looked for a new toy. *Anything you want*, I told him, and I watched his eyes widen at the sight of a miniature helicopter or car, his excitement making me believe, at least for a short time, that he was a child who might have enough. These were the moments I focused on, the scenes I chose to see, the way any mind in any situation convinces itself that tomorrow will be better.

We walked. We walked to escape the cold, but we were pinned down by its claws. I told myself we were meeting someone along this meandering path, someone who would take Jacob home, where there was heat, but this person was a hologram in my mind. John looked at me, then down at his son. He nudged his chin in his direction, then lifted his eyes to meet mine. *It will be okay*, I mouthed, and I realized I had become a person who uttered this absurd statement, how, when I was young, if someone had said this to me, I never would have heard it above the noise of my father's yelling, the inevitability of his leaving. I would have known better. But now, I wanted to believe these words, as I met John's gray eyes, still lighter than this dark sky, these clouds about to break open and release their wrath.

We were in the business of doing. There was seldom time to think. Inside the kitchen, John pulled baskets from grease, flipped meat on the grill, slid sheet pans from the oven within thirty second timeframes. I placed mounds of lettuce onto plates, garnished them with slices of tomato and carrot. We worked double shifts, fourteen-hour days of dashing past one another, the smell of wine and sweat, glasses clinking with ice as we scuttled into back rooms to smoke joints, to gulp shots of booze. On days when John had no time to leave the kitchen, he poured cooking wine into cups, drank vodka used for sauces from a straw. After we punched out, he hurried off toward what mattered to him most, and I was left waiting, wanting him.

In the evenings, when he returned, we stayed up for hours while most of the world slept. We talked and tossed underneath the covers, gave in to our inability to pull our hands from one another. We became preoccupied with skin. We guzzled wine from the bottle and watched one another by the light of candles. And I forgot about his disappearing and reappearing, my hoping that we would both be able to find a way out.

While we walked, the wind bit and stung my skin, my legs tingled with cold. John and I were accustomed to the chill, the sharp absence of relief; it had numbed us time and time again. But I felt guilty about Jacob's quiet cry, his knowing that everything and nothing would be okay. "Should we stop at the store to warm up?" I asked, pointing to the 7-Eleven on the corner.

"Not yet," Jacob said, his face serious. We headed over the bridge, crossed the river where teenagers hung out on skateboards in summer, above the nooks of wood and rock where they got high, and we glided across a parking lot, down a brick path that led to the restaurant where we worked, blasting into the back door of the kitchen. A haven of warm air rushed at us.

One of the servers crouched down to greet Jacob, hugged him before holding his face in her hands. "You're freezing," she said.

"I know."

Behind the chef's line, our co-worker dropped frozen chicken tenders in oil, the temperature cranked up high, the grease sizzling. "You hungry, buddy?" he asked, looking down at Jacob, who grinned, already beginning to tug on his coat sleeves.

John grabbed his apron from the shelf in the corner of the kitchen, reached to place it over Jacob's head, spun him around so he could tie it behind his waist. "The hat, too," Jacob said, and John took the snow hat from his son's head, replaced it with a white chef's hat sizes and sizes too big.

After Jacob had run around the kitchen with a spatula in his hand, taken inventory of the condiments in the fridge, talked with the chef about the best way to cook eggs, he followed us up the stairs to the lounge. We sat at a table near the bar and fireplace, and John cut the chicken tenders for Jacob, who received them piece by piece, smothering them in ketchup. When Jacob was finished with his food, we headed to the pool table, John lifting him up, guiding him on how to shoot, the balls clanging across the green felt. I sat and watched, tucked my knees up into my chest, sipped on my drink.

A new waitress, who I had only met once, approached me. Her long, braided hair extended to the top of her thighs. "It must be nice to have the day off. Especially with the little one and all," she said.

I smiled, but I did not correct her, didn't bother to tell her that Jacob was not mine, that his mother was out of the picture, that his father had a love greater than the two of us; because at this moment, none of it mattered. What mattered was that we were in a toasty room, with full bellies and satiated minds, that, for those minutes and hours, this little boy was filled with the pleasures of being young. That this finding of warmth had been within our control, when almost everything else was beyond our grasp.

PART III:
REMAINS

WHERE THE OCEAN
AND SKY DIVIDE

I haven't seen my father for several years. I no longer know exactly what he looks like. I carry a segmented picture of him in my mind, while other parts of him still remain, may always remain, a mystery. I see shadows of his thinning dark hair lightened by grays. I see the broad shape of his hands. My father's hands were olive toned with wisps of dark hair, without extra flesh and bulbous veins, never dry and wrinkly like my own, but strong and smooth. My father's hands were suited for an office—clean hands that handled paper, staplers, computers, and calculators. My father's hands were those of a few gold bands, each designed differently, reflecting the individual taste of the women who picked them out. I have constructed a picture of my father standing up with his back to me, gazing out a window, as if what he sees out there is the woman he is hypnotized by, the next woman he will have, the woman he'll allow to rework him like clay.

*

My father and Brenda kept *The Joy of Sex* on their nightstand. Their canopied bed was up against the wall by the entrance of their room, so if you opened the door even a crack, the book was the first thing you saw. Brenda left her see-through lingerie hanging on doorknobs and draped over closet doors. What she didn't leave out in the open, Jocelyn and I uncovered by snooping through dresser drawers: slinky satin with thongs attached, innocent looking nighties with holes for nipples to poke through.

We spent hours flipping through *The Joy of Sex*, studying the photos and cartoon-like drawings of the same couple who reappeared throughout the book. The woman wore a lacy, transparent bra, the man kissed her neck, her inner thighs, near her crotch, and she yelled in what appeared to be orgasm. I contemplated the action-like photos as if they were clips of movies, the thongs and nakedness and the sixty-nine position. I read the words vulva, vagina, and clitoris again and again, learned about how the penis was the most symbolic organ in all of history. There was man biting woman, woman biting man; there were Mardi Gras masks and flashes of rear entry. The man sticking his big toe into the woman's vagina reminded me of how when I sat on one end of the sectional couch while my father and Brenda were on the other, they took turns holding one another's feet in their hands while talking about reflexology pressure points, and smirked at each other.

*

After my parents divorced, my father picked me up for dinner on Wednesday nights. For years, this was the only time I saw him without Brenda. When we went to a sandwich or pizza shop, I'd order an Italian sub with all the cold cuts, provolone cheese, oil, and hot peppers. I'd eat an entire large even though less than half the sandwich filled my eight-year-old body, but I couldn't stop myself. I chewed without tasting my food, rushed to swallow like a prisoner who'd been starved for days. When I finished, I excused myself to the ladies' room to throw up. The abundance of food in my small stomach surged upward on its own. I spewed the undigested meats, tasted the oregano and basil more while regurgitating than while eating, the dryness of the heave leaving spices stuck to the back of my throat. I welcomed the burn of bile, the ability to release what my body had clung to as it went down—the sting of acid, the taste of salt and sugar—an act that would become as familiar to me as brushing my teeth, or emptying a full bladder. I remember how food had nothing to do with hunger.

Afterward, we sat in the booth like two strangers. "I got sick," I said. "I ate too much."

"Really?" he asked. I nodded while he kept chewing, blotted his face with a napkin. I expected him to ask me a question: "What were you thinking, ordering a sub the same size as mine?" or "Why didn't you cut it in half, bring the rest home?", but the conversation never went any further. He finished eating, folded the ends of the waxed paper, and wrapped the rest of his sandwich into a neat white package. I sipped from a bottle of water, swished it around in my mouth to rinse away the foul taste of vomit, feeling an indifference that came from being more familiar with my father's absence than his presence.

*

When my father dropped me off at home, I never told my mother about my puking. We didn't talk much about these dinners. Once he and my mother separated, he never walked up to the front door of the house again, only flew into the driveway and beeped, waiting for us to come out. One of these times when he pulled up to the house, he saw his best childhood friend helping my mother paint the garage, and said to him: "You have to choose. Her, or me. You can't be friends with both of us."

"Well if you're going to put it that way, I choose her," his friend said, and the two of them never spoke again.

After dinner, I went downstairs to the basement where my Barbies lived. I named them: Sherrie and Judy and Claire. Blondes, brunettes, a redhead. I orchestrated their dialogues, their arguments, heated fits of yelling, and their quiet, subdued apologies. I made up narratives about the houses they lived in, the Corvettes they drove, gave them each shots at being with Ken. I gave them whatever lives I pleased; they worked as waitresses and secretaries and teachers. They shopped at the mall, surfed at the beach, ate bananas and ice cream cones. They lived together in houses, forming large families of women, since there were so many of them, but only one or two Kens.

In secret, I played "naked Barbies." I ripped off their clothes, forced them to have sex with blond Ken and his brown-haired friend, though they all lacked the necessary parts to actually go through with it. The women took turns as I mashed them up against the one or two Ken dolls. I wiggled the plastic bodies, chafed their fake skin, bent their thin legs, rubbed them together like pairs of scissors trying to cut one another. Although the scenarios of their lives were completely up to me, each doll seemed to contain her own fire; I searched for meaning behind their stiff expressions—tried to detect something, anything that was real.

*

In fifth grade, I found out that the therapist my father sent me to in order to "help me deal with the divorce" was really supposed to have discovered why I was so fat, and to fix it. This was the same year I began to go for long stretches without food, feeling faint in the mornings before school and eating half an apple to make the dizziness subside. This was the same year I became diligent about doing Jane Fonda's workouts every afternoon, playing the video tape over and over, huffing on the living room carpet, even after my teacher took me out into the hallway and said, "Gina, it's nice to be thin, but not too thin." This was the same year that I refused to eat cheesecake on my birthday and Brenda, who was always talking about calories and fad diets, who in previous years had refused to let me eat in between meals, shook a bottle of Ex-Lax in my face and said, "You want to be like your sister?" This was the same year I became stricken with nightmares and insomnia so terrible that I often crawled into my mother's bed weeping in the middle of the night and when my father found out, he said, "I always knew your mom was a lesbian."

*

The next year, my father suggested that the two of us go for a walk after dinner. This was odd, since we rarely spent time alone without Brenda. We circled the neighborhood as the sun lowered behind the clouds. It was quiet except for the calls of the cardinals flittering over the pines and the heels of my sneakers scuffing against the pavement.

"Do you know how a man and a woman have sex?" he asked.

Startled by his question, I looked down and stared at my quickening feet, my sneakers' long, black laces scraping the dirt. "No." The lie came out naturally even though I hadn't had time to think about my response. It was as if the word "no" itself might somehow obliterate his question, as if its ability to oppose might muffle my ears and block out his voice.

"I'm talking about what they do physically—do you know exactly how it happens?"

I was not yet having sex, not even kissing boys or letting them grope me. Next year, I still wouldn't have my period, but I'd be smoking cigarettes and stealing Southern Comfort from package stores after school, drinking liquor and puffing on joints. I'd get into cars with boys I hardly knew, ride into the city with them, get stoned at their friends' houses, who I knew less, pass out in random places, wake up to cold cloths on my forehead in strange bedrooms.

I decided not to answer him, hoped that the silence might shrink me, that by pretending not to care, I might turn to ice and melt away. He said, "It's when a man's penis enters a woman's vagina." My face flushed, my pulse pounding in my ears. He wanted me to be sure of the specifics, the details and the exact precision of the body parts—one entering another—erection, penetration, ejaculation.

*

Later, I wondered why I feigned innocence with this man who, during my childhood, did anything but try to shelter me from the world. We watched *Jagged Edge*, where a woman was brutally raped and murdered, a graphic scene including the masked perpetrator slicing her nipples with a knife. We watched *The Accused*, where Jodie Foster was gang-raped on a pinball machine. I speculated about why I pretended to know nothing about sex with this man who would get held up in various parts of the country romancing women, extending two-hour airport layovers into days, this man who had already told me that he'd contracted gonorrhea, but who never warned me about the risks of sleeping around.

*

While watching *The Shining,* my sisters and I ran screaming from the living room when Jack wedged his face in between the broken wood and said, "Here's Johnny," with his open mouth and wide nostrils. There were parts of the movie I soon forgot, like the repeated scenes of blood pouring from the elevator, the chilling music, how the child with Extrasensory Perception could predict the hauntings of the place and the pernicious psyche of his own father. Of all the atrocious incidents, the part I distinctly remembered, the part from which all the others fell away, was when the dead woman emerged from the shower, a corpse who Jack passionately French kissed. On the reruns we watched, her body wasn't bruised or bloody the way it was on the uncensored version but disguised by the white silhouette of a naked woman. It was the seduction that I remembered. Even though her nakedness was concealed, at five years old, it was clear to me that the ghost was the familiar sight that preceded sex. As my father, unfazed, sat next to me on the couch and stared at the television, I saw a glimpse of what would become more lucid in the years to follow: it was impossible to know my father beyond the objects of his obsession.

*

When I was in college, my father said he'd never get married again. He stated this often during our frequent dinners, where our interactions were consistently awkward—me dropping a fork, him clanging a plate. We'd have drinks before our meals arrived, like old, estranged friends finally trying to break the ice.

"Is it wrong," he said, "to ask out a woman who just refused my best friend?"

"Yes."

"But she didn't want to go out with him."

"It doesn't matter," I said. "He's your best friend."

"You didn't even give it any thought."

"I don't have to. There's nothing to think about."

During these dinners, my drinks were never strong enough. I had long ago lost faith in my father being anyone but who he was: a boundless man who had always been too distracted, too self-absorbed to consider his kids, a man who asked questions but never listened to the answers, a man who I had no doubt would marry again. I was no longer interested in sifting through dresser drawers and closets, sniffing his wife's perfume, attempting to know him further by inspecting the essence of whomever he loved at the time.

*

When I was twenty-five, my sister called to ask if I remembered being molested as a child. "Do you think we were abused?"

"No," I said. "I don't remember anything like that."

What I did remember were the shadows of women on the walls in the houses where we lived, where we visited, in the rooms where we talked. I remember that when it came to sex, there were no rules, that boundaries were nonexistent, the way the ocean is formless, blending into the sky. What I remembered was how the first time I had sex, it was only to get it over with. It was with a boy I was friends with in his bedroom in broad daylight, his parents downstairs. I didn't feel much of anything—no pain and no blood and no pleasure—no wishes for it to continue or stop, no longing for it or denying it in the days afterward.

What I knew is that when I gave my five-year-old niece a bath, and she stretched her tiny arms, her skin softening with soap, suds splashing in the water, I imagined how she processed events, how she perceived the adults in her life. I wondered what she would remember from each year, what she would still be too young to absorb, which memories would take on the most weight as she grew older. It was something about her bathing, her nakedness, that provoked me to think this way, her innocence causing a dull aching below my waist. It was the opposite of sharp pain, but concentrated, centering itself in the middle of me, hollowness alongside heaviness, a presence I could not ignore. I sensed her fragility, her tenderness, and I became overtaken with urgency, an incessant need to protect her from anything that might, that could happen.

My father has no recollection of the instances I've described; I have confronted him about his senseless parenting, and his only reply has been, "I'm sorry—I really don't remember any of that."

I debate the power of memory itself—his, my sister's, mine—the way he has eradicated his while she and I have examined our lives, forming narratives from timeless moments, trying to interpret some sense of truth from an environment that often distorted it. In the end, my father's inability to look backward only widens the gap between us, separates us to the point of strangers; he's managed to erase our past encounters, as if we've never shared houses, ridden in cars together, or gone on trips. In the end, I presume we all depend on the only memories or voids we see fit—the flashbacks and half-truths that allow us to survive the impact of our losses.

*

The few times I saw my father beyond my college years, usually at a birthday party for my niece, I was curious about whether it would be the last time we saw one another. I was surprised by his growing a beard, gray with a few patches of black, or the way his stomach had rounded. I practiced nonchalance while Dawne offered small talk. He said nothing.

Afterward, I ruminated about the possibility that we might never make amends, knowing that if he died before me, I might feel irreparable regret, this worry turning into panic. Other times, I was insouciant, and became haunted by my lack of empathy, by my inability to connect with him, with the choices he has made. When you are abandoned by something you never really had to begin with, you don't feel the pain twisting itself into the depths of your gut the way it will when you experience an authentic sense of loss, the way your insides rip open when it becomes too painful to bear going on loving someone who has left. There has been no intimacy between my father and me, no letting go of reservations— our relationship has been coated with his capricious forms of nurture, my unsettled sense of security. In a way, there's a synchronicity to our ignorance of one another; he has spent a lifetime forgetting, while I have spent countless years trying to distinguish a distinct shape that is my father, to decipher a form that I have sprung up from, to find a line where the ocean and sky divide.

ON THE OUTSIDE

After John left for good, after I bounced from restaurant to restaurant, applied for various jobs available to someone with an English degree, woke up early to substitute teach before waiting tables and pouring drinks into the night, after moving into a new apartment across town where my mom helped me paint the kitchen walls red, after I began to feel like myself again, what became all too apparent was that I had never taken the time to slow down long enough to decipher exactly who that self was.

It was around this time that I found Corey's journal from his nineteen months in prison tucked away in my storage closet, on the floor behind Nanu's painting of a Native American girl with chubby chestnut cheeks. I flipped through the jade green book and faced the fluid handwriting slanted to the right like the slash button on a keyboard; the penmanship from the letters he sent me during those long months. The letters rested behind the journal, in the corner of the closet, up on a shelf. Hundreds of them. Some were sealed in freezer-sized Ziploc bags, while others sat in a bin folded into rectangular shapes, wrinkled with bits of paper torn off. He sent the letters on legal-size white pages with blue lines. Cursive, blue lettering ornamented them, and most notes began, *Dear My Guardian Angel.*

I don't recall when he began to address me this way, inscribing these words that implied a spirit who protects a person at all costs, who urges them to make the right choice when faced with two options— hitting another car head-on or crashing into a tree on the periphery of the road. While a person has no way of knowing which way to veer, somehow, by some miraculous intervention, they are saved.

*

When Corey was sentenced, we were twenty-one. We had been friends since our teen years, good friends, who'd grown up together experimenting with LSD, driving our first cars, going to proms and concerts, and hanging out at each other's houses after school. We built forts in the woods and stumbled around forests collecting firewood, went swimming in nearby lakes. We cruised the back roads of our hometown and huddled together in the cabs of parked trucks, passed CD cases with cut straws and dollar bills, inhaled dust that sped us up, that offered us respite from ourselves, took us far away from our longing until the sun blasted into the day.

On the day of his sentencing, I entered the court-house, and shuffled into the security line among jurors and defendants and clerical workers. I shook out my purse, dumping my wallet and ChapStick and keys into a gray bin, raising my arms while the guard patted me down.

Just before this last arrest for violating his proba-tion, Corey had slit his wrists. His aunt found him collapsed at the bottom of the basement stairs. An ambulance rushed him to the hospital and the doctors shocked him back to life, restoring his body except for a scar left on his chest from the burn. When he woke, officials dragged him off to prison, to the psych ward, where he sat in a cell with video cameras zoomed in, and the lights on at all hours, for two weeks.

In the elevator, I met Corey's lawyer, Tim. "Can you make sure he gets this?" I asked. I held out a sealed envelope with Corey's full name printed in large, black letters. The first letter. It began *Dear Beautiful Boy,* its words focused around perseverance and endurance, the will to live, a list of reasons to survive.

"No problem," Tim said, and shoved the letter into his briefcase pocket.

I wanted to ask Tim if Corey had arrived yet, or what he thought the verdict might be, but my throat felt obstructed. This drug charge, possession and transportation of three pounds of marijuana, was equivalent to three felonies. I blinked my eyes, trying to swallow the bulge. I could not cry. Not in the courthouse.

In the courtroom, I stood alone in the back row. I glanced around, searching for Corey's mother or brother, but saw no familiar faces. The bailiff's voice echoed, "Will everyone please rise?" The judge entered and banged his gavel. Defendants being charged with misdemeanors waited for their sentences. I grabbed onto the back of the bench in front of me as if it were a church pew. Two uniformed guards at the back of the courtroom pushed the double doors open, one on each side, leading the prisoners into the courtroom.

Corey shuffled in wearing a freshly pressed, green jumpsuit with a five-digit identification number patched on his shirt, and white sneakers. I didn't expect the shackles, and with their clanging sound, I grasped the bench tighter. He walked past me without looking up, and the guards pulled him two rows ahead. They held his elbows, leaving his hands without cuffs. White bandages wrapped each of his wrists.

His auburn hair hadn't been cut for a while, and it waved in various directions. He'd taken the silver studs out of his ears. Corey turned back just before the judge instructed him to stand, and his eyes caught sight of me. His face locked into mine, his lips still pursed, as if Tim had coached him on exhibiting an expressionless face. "Gina," he whispered, letting out a long breath. "My lawyer thinks they're going to give me sixteen months." He rushed by the words, spitting out the facts like mouthwash on a hurried morning.

Sixteen months. I tried to hide my surprise without looking down. I wanted to absorb his features and store them inside my mind—I didn't want to forget, the way we do when time passes—the way we will after going a long time without seeing someone.

"I gave your lawyer a letter," I said. "Make sure you get it."

"Okay." He looked down. "I didn't even see you here, Gina. I didn't know you were coming."

"I just wanted to see you. And I didn't know where to send the letter. I have to go now though. I'm missing a class—a quiz." I kissed the tips of the fingers on my right hand and then blew on them, lowering my hand as if offering communion.

"Thanks for coming."

"Write back to me," I said.

"I will." Corey winked, and turned back toward the front of the hollow sounding courtroom.

Sixteen months. I remember feeling it was imperative that he receive that first letter I'd written, the one that told him, *You are the strongest person I know*. I'm not sure if I believed this statement, but I believed in the power of language, of narrative—in the hope that my letters would keep him alive, or at least keep him from wanting to die. And like that, as I had learned to do from such a young age, I slipped into my role—this time of a supposed, celestial figure costumed with wings, who offered unconditional, inexhaustible love without a thought, who had no limitations when it came to depleting herself, who cared fiercely and without judgment, regardless of repercussions.

Outside, I tucked my hands into the pockets of my long, black coat. I bit my lip, tasted my raspberry lipstick. I'd worn makeup for the first time in years, not wanting to look like a convict's disheveled friend. The cold stung my face as I trudged through the snow to my car.

*

Page after page, Corey described his life behind bars—the people he met, some who seemed similar to us, who got into drugs as teenagers, then young adults, and took habits too far, trying to make extra dollars, and sinking instead into patterns of addiction. He avoided others, those being held for murder or pedophilia. In Corey's letters he explained the politics of prison—how it was its own little city, guards smuggling weed and cigarettes, men fighting in showers and hallways, yelling obscenities, giving one another tattoos with guitar picks. How when a man was convicted of child molestation, the other prisoners tortured him with shanks made from toothbrushes. Within months, he'd seen more heroin than he'd ever even conceived of outside prison walls.

During our phone calls, which were monitored, he alluded to the challenges of his daily life, like being stabbed in between the shoulder blades with a sharpened pencil during a shower, just before his watch was stolen. He described his daily routines—pull ups and kitchen duty, sharing meals with the other guys in the "chow" hall. Since we were always being listened to, I received the bits and pieces of his new life, and speculated my own endings. I hung up fraught with worry over the violence, other inmates setting him up for trouble, his loneliness. Other times, I could tell that he'd called not to talk, but to listen, to hear my voice; I told him about my classes, and I recapped college parties, insisting he wasn't missing anything worthwhile.

I scribbled pages encouraging Corey to push through this tumultuous time—to cooperate with the system and come out on the other side. My letters told him that he was not as misunderstood as he suspected, reiterating that jails were overpopulated with young males in their twenties dealing with drug charges. That prisons were unnatural. That people needed sunlight. I wrote to tell him about bumping into an old friend on campus who said, with surprise, that I looked much better than I used to. That the last time we saw one another was in high school, on the night of a football game, and I ran out of the woods covered with dirt and asked her if she knew where I could get some more acid. I told him that I knew how the world saw us, but that it didn't matter. In addition to my own writing, I sent Corey music and books: *Tuesdays with Morrie* and the new Phish CD. Intended for his time at the halfway house, I crafted a journal from recycled paper, and I filled in random pages with my own poems, as well as those of others. I pressed dried flowers into corners of the pages, and wrote an introductory dedication.

*

One evening, in my apartment, I answered the telephone, and heard the voice of an investigator. He was calling from the prison. "I need to ask you a few questions," he said.

I was sitting on top of a turquoise tapestry that draped my couch, but stood up at the urgency of his voice. Corey had been sending me money orders for months, but I hadn't thought much of it. They were made out to people I didn't know—I cashed some, sent others to different addresses, transferred money into his personal account. I figured he was playing poker, waging bets, passing time; I didn't fully understand the politics of prison, nor did I want to.

Halfway into the interrogation, I realized I shouldn't have agreed to talk with the investigator— I can still hang up, I thought, can say I have a baby crying, toast burning, anything. But I was not good at making excuses. I answered his questions honestly as he spouted off names and dates associated with the money orders. When I'd admitted too much,

I felt a pang of regret, my palms sweaty, my head tingling. I imagined Corey sitting in this man's office listening to my replies on speaker phone, cringing at the sound of my panic-stricken answers. I later found out that this was true. When we hung up, the officers sent Corey to the hole—a filthy, neglected cell where he sat by himself for twenty-three hours a day—no personal property except for a few sheets of paper and one book. They took away his phone and visitation privileges, and allowed him to shower only two times a week. Days passed without hearing from him, and then weeks. Finally, I called his brother to ask if he'd heard anything. "No, he replied. "But I'm done sending him money. I'm done doing anything for him."

*

When Corey's privileges were restored, I drove two hours north to visit him. I usually sat in my car and listened to Neil Young's "Comes a Time," but this time I stood on the sloped pavement and waited for the razor wire gate to open. Mountains towered behind the concrete walls, shadowing the early morning sky. When the hour turned, the guards released the automatic gate and waved us through. I shuffled in with the others, mostly women, many with young children. Inside, I opened my purse, presented my driver's license, raised my arms for the wand that scanned my body. I signed my name on the visitor's list, for which I was pre-approved. I held a Ziploc baggy filled with quarters for the vending machines. Long, plastic tables and oval seats lined the room, resembling the cafeterias in public high schools. I looked around at the other women, surmising the details of their relationships with the men they visited, wondering if the couples depended on these visits, and knowing that Corey and I did not. We had the letters.

In writing, Corey described the kind of citizen he wanted to be when released, a solid participant with hard earned responsibilities, with opportunities to travel, and to finally go to college. I responded with my own notions about the Peace Corps, about wanting to live in Ghana and Thailand and Italy, and then keep going. In letters, there existed a stream of consciousness that couldn't be contained, and I swallowed his words, ingested their palpable pulse. The words delivered bits of pleasure without completely satisfying, and as if on the brink of orgasm, I remained teased, in a dream-like state of wanting more.

He walked out from behind the heavy metal door in his green uniform, and I brought myself back to the harshness of our reality, of the present, away from the idealism of the words we shared, the hopes that seemed a billion years away. His curls had been cut off, and his face was serious, heading for me. I stood up and he pulled me into him, tight and close, my forehead pressed against his clean-shaven face. "I'm really sorry, Gina." I kissed him on the cheek, near the side of his mouth.

"It's okay," I said, and it was. Now that I saw his face. Now that I was not fighting tears while walking through the English building on campus, struggling up the stairs to my professor's office to tell her I couldn't make it to class that day, that I hadn't heard from my best friend who was in prison, that I was worried he'd try to hurt himself. She told me to take the day off. She gave me her home telephone number and said to call if I needed anything, no matter what time of night. She told me to go do the thing I did when my heart was breaking most. I went home and smoked a joint.

In the visiting room, Corey's eyes were direct and honest. He'd had a canned food business in jail—sold salmon and tuna and protein shakes, hoarding far more than the few each prisoner was allowed. He'd been smuggling cigarettes. He explained only minor details, since we were being watched. "Everyone does it," he said. "I just got caught. I'm sorry I risked our communication, that I couldn't write or call." I couldn't be angry with him. I didn't know the full extent of what it was like for him in prison; I assumed that he told me only a small piece.

It was no longer the way it was when he was on the outside, when we knew one another completely. Then, he could tell me about the things that bothered him: his intense loneliness, how his father refused to talk to him, how his parents slept in separate bedrooms, lived separate lives. How he'd been unable to express himself for years, until he'd found drinking and drugs. A year before, we'd have sat on the couch in my apartment listening to The Doors and smoking pot. He'd grab my journals from the shelves, flip through them, read passages, immerse himself in my life. He'd look up to see if I would stop him, knowing that I wouldn't. "I have nothing to hide," I'd say. We'd drink wine from a box and fall asleep sitting up, him eventually curling up on the couch next to me, his head resting in my lap—when we woke, things were silent and simple, with nothing to figure out, nothing to try to understand.

*

In the green journal, Corey had a long debate with himself about whether or not to tell me he was in love with me. He didn't want me to halt my life while waiting for him, but he couldn't deny it any longer. When he did tell me, in a letter, I was elated. I hadn't wanted to admit my mutual feelings. I was aware that being there when he needed someone most was an important job, and it was mine. That the unconditional love I gave shifted and shaped him. As I transitioned into womanhood, I was only a larger version of the famished young girl on an infinite search for a sense of something authentic, who'd become an expert at both deprivation and consumption—the girl who either denied herself altogether, or swallowed food without tasting, attempted to stuff herself with what was missing, to anchor herself to the ground, prevent her body from disappearing.

I became fixated with writing to Corey as if it were a guide to my survival. I waited for the influx of letters to arrive, from one apartment to the next. I stayed with a friend and her boyfriend one summer, and as soon as I moved in, she handed me the mailbox key. "Here, Gina. I know you'll need this." I existed as a writer locking herself in an upstairs bedroom while her roommates went to college parties without her. When I did attempt to be social, I'd drink too much, expose my sadness, and walk home alone, wishing I'd never gone.

During this time, I broke my foot running down the

stairs, and I had to wear a cast for two months. I was home alone, resting my injury, when the phone rang. I sat up and grabbed my crutches, but I couldn't move quickly enough. I heard the familiar recording come through the answering machine: "Hello, you have a collect call from an incarcerated inmate at Pond View Correctional Facility. Please listen for the inmate's name at the tone."

"Corey."

"Will you accept the charges?"

Silence.

Click. I missed it. I hobbled back over to the futon, buried my head in the pillow's fold, and sobbed.

Disappointment is a consistent, underlying emotion when you are in love with a prisoner. You must focus on optimism—on maintaining composure; to lose hope is to forego the promise of everything that will someday be yours, like giving up on the idea of a healthy infant at the end of a terrible pregnancy. When doubts about Corey and me crept up, I replayed and repeated our interactions by rereading the letters, and the written words between us sustained me. I used them to fill myself up.

*

After I found Corey's journal in my closet, I read about a woman's experience teaching in a prison classroom—about how the men became infatuated with her simply because she smiled at them, because she looked them in the eyes, these prisoners deprived of human contact, who'd take any attention available. And I wondered what I was thinking when I let myself fall in love with Corey. I know that I thought

I could redeem him—that I felt I needed him. And while his experience may have been congruous with the story of men in the prison classroom, what I realized later was that I was not dissimilar—a young woman whose greatest desire was to be desired, who was reverting back to fitting a preconceived mold she'd stepped into as a child and then refuted for years, falling into a familiar pattern of loving men who did not have the capacity to love her back. I tried to understand this romance fueled by letters, by distance, by impossibilities. After it was over with Corey, and then with John, I began to examine my tendency to latch on to unobtainable men like a rock climber strapped into a harness, holding on as if any moment, one slip could alter my life, or take it; I could fall and tumble and break apart.

In writing and receiving the letters, I felt a galvanic kick, electricity I had not known in conversation, no matter how deep. I pictured Corey's hands, callused from hours of shoveling snow in the prison yard. I saw his hands folding the letters, stuffing them into envelopes. I envisioned his hands on my body. I realized later that it was the absence of these men that made me crave them more, the constant possibility of losing them—the threat of my not being able to save them. It was similar to how the most intense sex is the kind we don't know when or if we'll have again—how inside uncertain moments, we experience an urgent intimacy.

*

Corey was released on a damp, August day, and I drove to the halfway house with my truck's windows rolled down, the radio playing U2. I drove not really believing we were about to see one another outside of protected walls, away from security cameras and white lined paper. I drove knowing that our words would resonate in the humid air, that without barriers, we would fulfill our physical desires. After I picked him up, we rode an hour to my apartment, his duffel bag between us, and his hand tucked underneath it, holding my bare thigh. I had sautéed chicken tenders and baked eggplant parmesan, the food spread across the dining room table. We left it, still warm from the oven, and lay down on the sofa—Corey's first contact with home furniture in almost two years. He took off his shirt, his chest shining with sweat, strong from weightlifting, his skin brown from working outside on construction sites all summer. We kissed, timid at first, then long and hard, my hands on his back, him on top of me, moving his lips downward.

When he glided his tongue up the inside of my thighs, I said, "Do you think it's too soon?"

He laughed. "More like not soon enough."

"I know," I said, and I climbed on top of him, my body collapsing around him, our skin sticking, our flesh fitting together.

*

Post-prison, Corey lived in his parents' house in our hometown, still without a driver's license because of his record. He drank heavily, more heavily than before his arrest, as if trying to make up for the year-and-a-half loss. One night he called me at 3 a.m., crying. "Can you come over?"

I drove the hour south to his parents' house. By

the time I got there he was passed out, so I crawled into bed with him. The next day, when we woke up, his mother said, "Gina, if he goes anywhere today, it needs to be an AA meeting."

"I know," I said, emphasizing the second syllable. "I completely agree."

Her cheeks sunk down with surprise. She believed I condoned his alcoholism, as if I didn't realize he'd lost a chunk of his life. As if I hadn't been waiting nineteen months for him. As if I hadn't reduced my life to filling notebooks and cards, to waiting impatiently for mail to arrive. She was still used to me being his corrupt sidekick, and I couldn't blame her—I did understand his need to break free from rules and restrictions, but I also understood his need to break free from drinking, from drugs. I was willing to do whatever I could to help keep him sober, stable, and most importantly, out of jail.

Corey habitually planned to meet me, but got sidetracked with old drinking buddies and forgot to call; he passed out at random apartments with his phone turned off. He downed bottles of Captain Morgan and in turn forgot the endless pages he'd written, the newfound epiphanies and motivations he'd had. I allowed him to consume my life while locked up, and now, without the letters, I was becoming as lost as he was. The agony grew thicker—the continuous stress of his unavailability despite his freedom gathered in my gut. Now free, he spoke to me in riddles— claiming to want to spend time with me, then turning careless, forgetting that we had forged a union, that I had postponed my life.

I grew tired. I questioned the truth of the months

and months of letters. For nearly two years, I'd held on to the promise of what would someday be mine— glimpsed it, grazed it, touched it. One night Corey called to say he was hanging out at an apartment down the road with some old friends, but he wasn't sure he'd be stopping by. I paused on the other end and said the thing I didn't want to say, but that I knew to be true: "It seems pretty clear that you don't want to be in a relationship."

"You're right, Gina. I won't be ready for a relationship for quite some time."

*

The night Corey offered me the green journal, eight months after his release, he delivered it an hour north, to where I lived, where my roommates were hosting a party for me because I was moving to California. Corey showed up at the house and waited for a chance to give me the book. After almost everyone had either left or gone to sleep, I sat on the sofa with John, whom I'd recently begun dating. Corey sat across from us and passed a joint. His green eyes followed it to my lips. Then, he reached into his backpack and grabbed the book. "I want you to have this, Gina. I came here to give this to you."

"What? What is it?"

"It's my journal. From prison."

"Why do you want to give this to me? I don't want it."

"Please, just take it. It's all for you. I want you to have my thoughts." I wanted to say no again. I wanted to tell him, "This journal is your life—your words—it doesn't belong to me. It never belonged to me." But sitting across from him, and next to John, I simply accepted it to lessen the awkwardness.

Afterward, I considered returning it. I envisioned mailing it to his parents' house. But I kept it. I did not read it before I drove west, and I did not take it with me to California, the place I was going to relieve myself of my mistakes. I don't remember when I began to flip through it, only that it was years later. And, when I opened it, I reacquainted myself with the cursive handwriting, with the aspirations, the confusions, the admissions of truth—with the reality that the writing was all about me.

*

Now, I see it this way: if you are imprisoned, in order to survive, you must focus on an attraction that will pull you out. And like a mistress, I served as Corey's escape, his daydream, the place where he was not restrained. I had been the drug. Like a secret lover, I embodied freedom, his space away from misery. And I, too, used him as a distraction from looking inward, from dealing with the fact that even though I was no longer using drugs, I had no real sense of who I was, or where my life was going—that I was still unable to hear anything beyond the echo of my father and Brenda's voices as they berated me. That, over the years, I had slipped so far into myself that my body felt boundless, an immeasurable cavern I might slide into before breaking apart and dissolving.

*

I traveled back into Corey's journal, questioning the sincerity of the relationship. One aspect that occurred to me is that the more time passed, the more his writing had begun to resemble my own. It was as if my words articulated a script and he rehearsed it—I became the unintentional ventriloquist. I'm not sure when or how this happened, or if he noticed it at all—if he truly believed what he said, or absorbed it by repetition, by the need to survive.

My memory of these few years, the years with Corey and then John, continually reinvents itself. Now, I contemplate Virginia Woolf's quote about the illusion of love, about it being "a story we make up in our mind about another person." And it's true that when you are waiting for a person to be set free, you are forced to create a character to fill the void. But what is also true is that I was making up a narrative of who *I* was, too, by accepting and embracing a label indicative of an otherworldly being, letting myself be identified by a title that would set me up for failure again and again.

I know what seemed real when Corey was in prison: our love, and what seemed real after his release: our illusion. But perhaps I am looking for too much distinction. A way to avoid or deny or make sense of the raw and honest moments between two people who have known the many dimensions of one another.

I look at the journal on my living room floor, and I realize, even though so many years have passed, I am no closer to knowing what to do with it. *Maybe I will send it to Corey*, I think. Or maybe I'll throw it away. Or maybe it will remain untouched for another decade, on the bookshelf, and I will forget.

THE DRESSING ROOMS

I have gone too long without describing my mother. My mother, whose scent is of dryer sheets mixed with jasmine and geranium, who, for years has been stopped in stores and at gas stations and malls to be told that she looks like Rhoda from the 1970s TV sitcom, *The Mary Tyler Moore Show*, played by Valerie Harper—that her dark hair and long eyelashes, the shape of her eyes and wide smile all point to this resemblance. I have always wanted my mother's hands—her long fingers with well-defined knuckles, the kind she complains about not being able to fit her rings over, her smooth, lotioned palms, the skin of a woman who grooms and maintains— this hair plucked from the body, that earring clasped, these panty hose slipped up and over legs.

After her mastectomy, when my mother was wheeled from surgery into recovery, the IV poking her hand, it was easy to forget that she needed whatever they were injecting her with—Percocet or morphine or Dilaudid. I wanted the nurses to pull the IV from her vein, to leave her hands alone, to finally let this small part of her rest. They itched. The rest of her did, too, her free hand poking around her chest, scratching at a phantom breast no longer attached to her body. Her hands remembered. These hands that held babies to breast and filled bottles with milk, spooned mushy food into hungry mouths, that kneaded endless dough, dropped breaded chicken and eggplant into sizzling pans. These were the hands of diamonds and wedding bands, of having held small bodies as they scurried across the street, of weary, tireless work, of scrawling chalk across a blackboard, stitching and sewing children's clothes, of building a computer for a final school project at the age of fifty. They were the hands that touched and fed a husband who fled, the husband she mentioned now, high from the Percocet or morphine or Dilaudid.

The nurse adjusted the IV that dripped liquid into her vein, mixed with her blood, while my mother asked perpetually, constantly about the itch, and the nurse insisted she could not do anything more for her. "It should go away in twenty-four hours," she said, as if that was answer enough. And as my mother's eyes fluttered, opened and closed, I became overtaken by anger, staring intently at the nurse, who was only doing her job, a job of saints, and I thought about words that might rip through her, violent words I didn't know I was capable of thinking—this instinctual, uncontrollable urge, this surge to protect. *This is what a mother must feel for a child*, I thought. A friend once told me, "It's as if you'd step in front of a train for them in an instant. You wouldn't even pause to think about it."

In my late thirties, I had never had an urge to procreate, to have a body growing inside my own, attaching itself to the deepest parts of me. But at this moment, I would stand in front of a train for my mother. I would yell at the nurse to kill her pain, question the meds she administered, refute the plastic surgeon who thought she could do the work of God, hold them all accountable for this loss of her breast, for the cancer invading the same body part for the second time, after she had already done her time, her six weeks of radiation, where I accompanied her on Fridays, surrounded by men and women in johnnies and socks, people reading *Time* and *Cosmopolitan*, and drifting off into distraction.

The first time, each Friday, in the waiting area, my mother and I talked about recipes— haddock smothered in crushed walnuts and Italian style greens with garlic and onion, chicken picatta with olives. We talked about her friend who had just flown in from New Mexico, how they went to their favorite bargain store, where they sometimes bought the same outfits since they lived so far away from one another. My mother asked the technician with the jet black, shining hair what her kids dressed up as for Halloween, smiling wide at her responses, *witch* and *pumpkin*. "How cute," my mother said.

We sat in a room where we uttered what seemed like every word except for "cancer," a word that made my body twinge with uncertainty, with the possibility of devastation. In the waiting area, I prattled in my head, placing bets about what kinds of cancer invaded the bodies underneath the gowns, while chapel interns kneeled by us, praying, as they looked up at my mother with her jeans under her gown, her colorful platform shoes, her hydrated, flawless complexion, her clusters of freshly curled hair.

During these weeks of radiation, I didn't tell my mother that I felt as if I was locked inside someone else's skin waiting to be let out. That my world seemed smaller. That when I was at work, I glided across the carpet as if walking on air, serving elderly patrons hot pastrami melts and gin martinis, and I wondered how they'd made it this long. That I thought of her, who ate beet greens and organic meats and exercised daily, and my anger rose. Why was it *she* who was inflicted, why *her* and not them? To my mother, I said, "They caught it early. You'll be fine."

*

This time, after the mastectomy, while sitting at an intersection of windowless hallways for hours, gazing at rows and rows of doors lining each corridor, I had the stifling feeling I first experienced as a toddler after losing my mother in the grocery store. I'd wandered around until somebody decided to help, to sound out my mother's name over an intercom for everyone to hear. It was a feeling I went on to have for years, becoming exacerbated in steamy showers where I'd wheeze for several minutes until finally catching my breath. It was more than loneliness, than isolation; it was a feeling of somehow being invisible and transparent at the same time, of sinking and slipping, of falling away.

This time, after the nurse and the IV, after the wound that would not heal because of scar tissue from the radiation, after the necrosis of the skin, the blood that refused to flow through tissue that turned black, after the plastic surgeon admitted she was not God, I would chastise them, I would correct them. I would urge her to forget, to forego the reconstruction of the breast. When her infection lasted months, my sister and I cooking and delivering daily meals, washing her hair, my stepfather giving her meds and changing her bandage, she would have no choice but to comply. During this time, I would realize I could not save my mother, in the same way every parent must receive this crucial lesson for a first time—the way my mother surely received it when it came to me, although she would try and try and try. She would yell from the doorstep to "put a helmet on" as I took off on ATVs with the neighborhood boys, her voice trailing behind me in the distance, she would switch from job to job, rearranging hours and shifts in order to be home to let me in after school, to monitor where I was, demand that I go to a therapist during my high school years.

And later, she would trudge alongside me through the college campus in snow, our pants and ankles wet, lugging suitcases of clothes into the elevator, plastic storage totes on top of one another, her bag packed with Nutri-Grain bars and homemade hummus and lentil soup, while offering suggestions to cope with my list of debilitating fears, which was becoming longer and longer. I was afraid of cleaning chemicals, especially bleach, accidentally ingesting lead paint, an odd lump on my skin, ink poisoned blood from pen scratches near major veins. I had become obsessed with death, with the finality of it, afraid of the earth or sky swallowing me. I suffered from intense insomnia, and when I did fall asleep, I woke up in the middle of the night alarmed; I had dreamt of my sister dying, or a faceless man holding a gun to my head. And still, my mother's tender words, her signing me up for workshops and classes, for support groups, her insistence on going with me, on driving me there, could not pluck these thoughts from my mind.

After my mother's infection cleared up, her wound finally healed, her cancer gone, we would shop for a prosthesis, and I would follow her through the small shop outside of Boston like the five-year-old girl in Loehmann's department store all those years ago, when I was reminded that my mother was the most beautiful woman in existence, in her blue blouse and white skirt, the red flats left on the dressing room floor. That she would always be what's left.

It's Not What
It Looks Like

B renda used to park the car on Locust Street
and turn off the engine. We'd examine the red
house while we sat out front by the mailbox. "This
is the house," Brenda would say. "This is where that
asshole killed his wife. *Look* at it."

In my memory of these trips, I am twelve years
old. Seventeen years later, at almost thirty, while in
graduate school for creative writing, I drove to the
small, southern New Hampshire town where my
father and Brenda had lived, to research my youth.
I passed the old barn, now converted into a convenience store, and rode by Frederick's Family Diner.
I veered off the main road remembering, without a
doubt, the sharp left onto Locust Street, even though
I never actually lived in this town.

The ranch-style house wasn't painted red any
longer. Aluminum siding concealed it. The new
owners chose a brownish yellow color. The color of
khaki pants.

*

Pulled over on the right side of the road, Brenda's
long, slender nose used to point at me as she glared

out the passenger window. My spot in the passenger seat was close to the mailbox, as if I were delivering a small parcel from the car's window. Or a message. Brenda's wheat-colored hair frizzed out at the ends, with dark roots exposed closer to her scalp. The car was positioned so that if the door opened, she could push me right out onto the lawn. But she didn't do this. Instead, she narrated. "He used to beat the shit out of her. Bruise her up and bite her and punch her. Over nothing. Probably nothing." She didn't shake her head in disgust, but stayed sedate, as if waiting for me to shake mine.

But I didn't flinch.

She said, "And then finally..." Her wide eyes zoned in on me, then the house. She smiled with her mouth closed, a firm and defining smile, as if no more words were needed—the story was legible.

*

Seventeen years later, the new occupants used the same mailbox. Black iron with a red flag, and the gold number seven. It was far more rusted than I remembered, the black paint chipped to expose metal, browned and golden from years of snow and rain. This mailbox had towered in the yard because no trees surrounded the house, and they still didn't—it was just like before, as if Locust Street marked a barren desert in the middle of the small New England town. No life pronounced itself there.

*

The first time at the dead end on Locust Street, I asked Brenda, "Did you know him? Or her?" The only similar crime I'd heard of was the famous Pam Smart case, the one where the high school teacher in a coastal New Hampshire town had an affair with one of her students and then hired him to kill her husband. But it was still different—a distant murder, as opposed to severing your spouse's life with your bare hands.

"No," she answered. Brenda didn't say how she'd heard about the murder, whether from the newspapers or town locals. She didn't say the names of the man or his wife or indicate that she even knew what they were. She didn't say why we went out of our way to visit the house. And I never asked.

I didn't recall the residence having been a duplex, but I did remember the shutters, broader around the windows' top halves, spread wide like butterflies' wings. I recalled wondering about the poor woman who lived behind the windows. I pictured her sweeping up dirt on the kitchen floor while her husband, with a red, windburned face and scaly knuckles, pointed his finger and hollered, his words flying with drops of spit. I sometimes envisioned her alone, secretly wanting to hit him over the head with the broomstick, and other times I saw her with a baby she was trying to protect from him, the murderer. In my thoughts, he turned the stove's burners up high and held her fingertips there to scorch them. In my thoughts, she screamed.

"How did he kill her?" I asked. "Did he shoot her?"

"No, the asshole just bruised her up the way he always did, but this time it went too far and she died. Maybe he pounded her face in and damaged her brain or something. Think about it."

I didn't want to think about it, but I couldn't help seeing the woman's face as a resemblance of John Hurt's in *The Elephant Man*. Seeing her flat on the floor with pieces of brain oozing out her forehead. I was sorry I'd asked. I was only attempting to fill in the silence, but each time she responded, my skin grew warm to the touch as if my blood were simmering. Our voices could not deter me from Brenda's wild and focused eyes, pinballs darting back and forth between the house and me.

*

The house was not situated in a neighborhood one would just drive by—it was at the end of the road, but there was no cul-de-sac. No turnaround, a dead end. The pavement just stopped there. You had to go out of your way to get to it.

After driving down this street, no more than a half mile long, I looked for myself there, for the girl I had been at age twelve. Long, dark hair and hollowed-out eyes. Dark circles. Straight-faced. I expected to see Brenda's car waiting at the end, as if part of a painting. But I only saw the house staring back at me.

An open bag of kitty litter rested on the doorstep of the khaki-colored ranch. The hedges leaned out from under the windowpanes. They were trimmed, not perfectly, but well enough. The couple's driveway had been on the right side of the house, where a motorcycle now parked. Their driveway started out narrow and grew wider as it got closer, like the house was about to suck you in.

*

Brenda's hands were masculine, with thick fingers and unpainted fingernails kept short. Her hands were so large that I thought it would only take one of them to smother my entire face. But instead, they held onto the steering wheel as if ready to whip to the right and drive through the front of the house.

The car's leather interior made my stomach churn. It was a smell somewhere between rubber and plastic. The scent was artificial, like a chemical cleaning spray that gives you a pounding headache. It nauseated me. The leather stuck to my skin, and I felt flushed with warm air, even when the heat wasn't on. It was stuffy, like the recycled air on a plane. Surrounded by leather, I would crack my window as soon as I got in. I needed oxygen.

Brenda was an investigator, and I her forced accomplice. I never spoke enough to tell her to stop taking me there, but she was not the kind of woman you felt you could speak to—you simply went along with her because there was no other place for you to go. She was not the kind of woman you felt you could listen to—you had to let her words bounce off you like pebbles grazing a river. She was not the kind of woman you could argue with—it was better to appease her so you might slip between the cracks and out of her sight.

I didn't want to imagine the woman who lived inside the house, her bloody body and the husband who beat her. I wanted to leave the structure as an ordinary house in an ordinary neighborhood. I wanted to erase its significance. "This is where it happened," she'd say. "Psycho bastard."

In the days between dragging me to this house,

Brenda became consumed by other cryptic obsessions. She told me about a haunted house where blood dripped out of the kitchen faucets. It was real. She'd read books about it. *We could go there if I wanted to. To Rhode Island.* She often mentioned a local kidnapper who'd been snatching children up into his white van and driving away with them. *Think about it. It's easy to lift a kid who only weighs eighty pounds, like you. You'd better be careful.*

These other memories were fleeting, like conversations once had or beers once gulped, but it was this house, formerly red, that continued to invade my mind. The others I had to dig to retrieve, while this house visited me unexpectedly time and time again. I woke up stiff with nightmares where the front door was ajar, the curtains open, and I was left to debate about what I'd find on the other side of the walls, but I never moved any closer. I didn't make it onto the brittle grass or the widening driveway—I didn't come close to getting inside. I stayed by the car, looking back and forth, trying to decide where I might find solace. Then I woke up.

*

My mind, I have found, is a patchwork quilt—certain sections are threadbare, dull and faded, gray, worn corduroy alongside other printed, busy fabrics, like star patterns or rainbow plaid. The bold pieces stand out. I'm uncertain why some memories have flashed like these loaded squares, gripping me relentlessly, while others have existed as undercurrents, only tugging gently. The red house was a recurring tidal wave that crashed over and soaked me, giving my flesh more weight.

I have written of our stalking the red house habitually because this is how I remember it. But now, I speculate. What if this was an isolated incident that has simply become a prominent recollection? What if one single outing has become dispersed in my mind so that I recall segments surrounding it? What if my memory of Brenda has simply *become* this house?

I imagined a shag carpet inside, in the front room, pea green and stained with cat feces. The two of us perched on leather seats, Duran Duran's, "Hungry Like the Wolf," playing through the speakers, like in the movie starring Farrah Fawcett, where she blared this song on her car's stereo just before driving her children to a field where she shot them because she was obsessed with a man who wanted nothing to do with them. Her character was not dissimilar from Brenda, an infatuated woman driven to darkness, compelled by a task she was determined to execute. The singer spoke of chasing a woman, and there we sat, watching the house where a man conquered his own prey. Brenda, like Farrah Fawcett, seemed starved.

"Is he in jail?" I remembered asking. Brenda responded that the husband had been arrested, arraigned, and sentenced. I didn't know whether to believe her or to worry he was peeking out the window at us from behind those ancient lace curtains, stained with splotches of brown; with Brenda, each day was like fumbling down a dark hallway unsure of where it led.

*

I had spent seventeen years fearing red houses, but now the house was brownish yellow. It used to seem hours away from the bordering town where I lived with my mother, like an enormous gated mansion on the top of a hill with a long driveway, but now it was small and dingy, as slight as an alleyway between city buildings.

I imagined that by driving here, moments would collide into a perfectly construed explanation, molded like a clay structure on exhibit at the local museum. I imagined that I'd remember the house before being able to regurgitate it. To purge it. But peering at the siding and the rooftop so many years later, I felt nothing. I had arrived with the notion that I'd feel something dramatic, but like having a tooth pulled without cringing, I was anesthetized. I questioned whether it was my memory that was unreliable— was I even at the right house? I never knew the exact address until today, but I did remember how to get here. At age twelve, in front of this house, I didn't feel like an almost adolescent, but like someone older who might have to jump out of the car and run through the woods to get to the main road and hitch a ride to anywhere else.

Seven Locust Street. Now, I took notes while I sat in front of the house. My car had a soft cloth interior. I leaned my cheek against the headrest. It smelled musty and familiar. Comfortable. My car was pulled over to the right, but this time I was strapped into the driver's seat, in command. The house struck me differently from this position. I didn't fear the house. It was one of those moments where expectation exceeds reality. It was one of those moments where you question who you are and whether you still resemble the person you were seventeen years prior.

I reached for my cell phone and dialed the town's police department to ask about the murder that occurred on Seven Locust Street. "Around the year 1990, the one where the man murdered his wife after battering her for years. The domestic homicide? Do you remember what I'm talking about?"

"I don't remember anything like that," the dispatcher said. "Hang on a minute. Let me make sure." I heard muffled sounds and people talking back and forth. "No, I've been here twenty years. I haven't heard of anything like that. You must have the wrong town."

"Are you sure?" I asked. "Not even around the year 1990?"

"No, I'm positive. I just confirmed it. There has never been a murder like that in this town or on that street. You really must have the wrong town. The wrong state."

I held the phone in my hand for a few minutes after the dispatcher hung up.

Maybe the dispatcher is wrong.

Or maybe I was simply chaperoned by a lunatic. I had no doubt that Brenda was a mendacious woman, but why would she have lied about *this*? What would be the point?

The phone call revised my childhood. There was an element of stillness to my surprise, a slight indifference, as if the man on the other end of the line told me I was adopted, and even though I hadn't been aware, it was something I had always suspected in a small corner of my mind. As if I showed no physical resemblance to my parents, but it had gone unmentioned, the same way Brenda's instability went unspoken. The imaginary world merged with the actual, but perhaps the former was more pertinent than the latter, especially when it was all I'd known.

In front of the house, I wondered how the choices I'd made as an adult had been affected by its presence in my life. I thought about the nonprofit work I did for an organization to prevent violence against women and also to support the victims. I worked on a crisis line, trying to talk women through survival, women similar to the one I believed lived on Locust Street. It was difficult to believe she never existed, her dark eyes and puffy skin. I wondered who really lived there when we used to sit outside. Perhaps it was a young and healthy couple, with glowing skin. With twin children or a golden retriever or both. Or maybe it was an elderly couple who'd been married for nearly a lifetime, keeping one another company in old age. Perhaps Brenda did know the people who lived there and asked them to stay inside for a while so she could play a trick on me. So the house would look deserted.

*

When I revisited this house, I didn't know Brenda any longer. After nine years of marriage, she and my father divorced. He explained that they had been "partners" for most of their marriage, and that they became strangers before their separation. That she pulled away from him before finally asking for a divorce. He described her as having become a zombie, a woman doped up on Prozac and Percocet. "She started starving herself and walking around expressionless," he said. *She was expressionless anyway*, I thought. That tight smile. Those unfazed lips and eyes. That stoic face staring into the house's paint and wood, penetrating its walls and piercing its foundation.

After divorcing my father, I heard that Brenda had an affair with a construction worker with three young children, whom she planned to marry. A stepmother again. I wondered about the lies she might have told those children. I wondered how they might discover the truth on their own, how they might differentiate reality from fantasy.

We saw Brenda one time after the divorce, my father and I, at a lawyer's office where she worked. She was standing outside when we arrived, staring at us. "Don't look," he said. She sucked hard on a menthol cigarette, even though we'd never known her to smoke. She looked thinner and wore a black knee-length pencil skirt and strapped high heels. She looked like a business executive or a private detective. She looked like someone I'd never met. She could have been anyone, except for her stare. Brenda gaped at us. Through us. Her cigarette smoke wafted up as we turned to enter the building—it circled around like a thick storm cloud trying to capture me.

Years after my father and Brenda divorced, I searched for her online and found out that she served on the board of directors for a familial organization that provided education in the community. The nonprofit organization offered parenting tips, prevented child abuse, and was meant to improve the lives of people and families. Brenda was also a *guardian ad litem,* which meant the fate of unknown kids was in her hands. When I read the description of Brenda's job, it reminded me of a girlfriend in high school whose dad I believed to be a kind-hearted family man, the only father I was comfortable alone in a car with, until one day in the bathroom at school, she lifted up her shirt to show me bruises and bite marks, the remnants of his morning routine. *It's not what it looks like.*

*

I knew I would never turn down this road again. I knew it in the way one knows it is time to leave a long-term lover—in the way it doesn't need to be said—the relationship has died, and your words are all used up. It no longer makes sense to salvage the connection.

I turned the key in the ignition and drove away from the ordinary khaki house. I turned off Locust Street and onto the main road, toward the interstate. I was on my way home.

THE DREAMING
AND THE WAKING

When I finished graduate school and became more and more serious about my writing, having learned how to spend long hours alone inside the shell of my body without thrashing forward, flinching back, without fighting or running, I decided to take a trip to Santa Cruz, California, the city that I escaped to that crucial summer after Nanu died nine years before. It was a city that epitomized the dreams I'd always had of the west, bubbling over with diverse liberals, political speakers, those advocating women's choices and Greenpeace. Where I found a summer sublet in a Jewish co-op, although I knew little about Judaism or kosher food, the only type allowed in the house, and where I answered a job advertisement that stated: *Laid-back people wanted. Casual dress, tie-dyes welcome. Work for a local art company.*

In the summer of 2002, after I'd left the east coast, I was unable to shake the words of a close friend who'd told me I was "spiraling downward." I stopped drinking and smoking, and I gave up caffeine. I kept myself busy by making root teas and consuming immune-boosting herbs each day. I'd hoped to find some clarity through the haze that my life had become, thought that by leaving, I might be able to decipher my masochistic tendencies—my spending two years waiting for Corey; my recent involvement and infatuation with John.

Nine years later, when I returned to Santa Cruz, I drove to the ocean. I walked along West Cliff Drive, a stretch of pavement that hugs Monterey Bay; I used to run this path each day after work, and watch the sun melt into the sky. I was still mesmerized by the redwoods, the lighthouses. The morning fog was an old friend I'd forgotten about, but when I saw her, she greeted me as if no time had passed. Sequoias and cypress trees stood close to the cliffs, their roots buried in the succulent grass, their trunks surrounded by yellow island bush poppies. People sat in their cars and stared out at the sea. When I lived here, I was afraid of forgetting Nanu. I tried to remember each detail: the clicking sound his jaw made when he cleared his throat, the way he rubbed his eyes like a child when he took his glasses off and rested them on the coffee table for the night, the delicate way he held the decanter when he poured himself a scotch, his voice following the clack of the pool's gate when he opened it each day at noon during our visits to Florida. "I think it's time for a glass of vino girls. What do you say?" That summer, I sat on the cliffs over the water watching the sun retreat into the sky, the mist spraying my bare feet, and I felt the heaviness of my body. I hoped the ocean would heal me, that the grief that had become part of me would slide down and dissolve into a fault in the mudstone, that the salt air would carry with it a feeling of relief.

At the art company, I became a receptionist. My

job description entailed playing the Grateful Dead on a boombox and "shooting the shit" with people waiting for interviews one or two days a week. On the non-interview days, alone in the office, I answered phone calls in between practicing yoga on the floor or working on poems and vignettes at my desk.

Some days my boss, Rick, was in the office too. He was blond, blue eyed—a thick Ken doll with a short haircut and fair skin. He fit the stereotype of a salesman; he talked about "expanding the company," "business booming," said things like, "my top guy brings home six figures a year." He'd leave the door to his office open and call to me: "Gina, come here for a minute."

One of these afternoons, I walked into Rick's office and he nodded to the chair on the other side of his desk. "Sit down—hang out for a few."

His office was sparse. The walls were naked except for a couple of prints that the company sold: Van Gogh's *Sunflowers* and Picasso's *Mediterranean Landscape*. The entire place was almost empty, as if a real estate agent was going to appear any minute to show the vacant property. Rick's desk was clear, no pens or papers or books—as if he had nothing to do when the employees were out in the field.

I sat across from him sipping chamomile tea. Rick sat behind his desk, his hands folded on top of it as he hunched forward. "I had two girlfriends once."

"What do you mean?"

"For a few years. I dated them both. I'd hang out with one on one day and another the next. It was tough, a lot of work having two women."

"And you pulled it off for *years*?"

"They eventually found out. I never knew how, but they called one another and decided to set me up. I was supposed to pick one of them up, Teresa, and it turns out Sheila—that was the other girl's name— she showed up at Teresa's house too. I pulled in and saw them both standing there on the front lawn."

"So what did you do?"

"Well, naturally, I started backing out of the driveway and went home. I figured I was busted."

"Interesting," I said. "Sounds like a bad romantic comedy."

"Yeah, it was a pretty bad idea. They were both so pissed. But, it was fun while it lasted. And I really did like them both." He smiled, showing his straight teeth, and no sense of remorse. I didn't think his story was funny, but I laughed at the ridiculousness of it. I thought it unkind but I wasn't there to make friends, and I certainly wasn't there to judge anyone else's mistakes. I only wanted to sort through the mess that was my past.

When the conversation paused, Rick opened his desk drawer and pulled out a cloudy baggy, emptied the white powder onto the desk. "Want some?" he asked.

I wasn't surprised, since salespeople often reminded me of the crews in restaurants—people who worked their asses off all day and then partied hard at night. When my co-workers came back to the office at the end of the day, I refused invitations to this bar or that party; I made up excuses about having to go running or meet my roommates, but sometimes, I simply spoke the truth, said, "I came here to try to clean myself up." It was bizarre to hear these words

come out of my mouth, as if I were an AA spokesperson
or an authority on sobriety when the truth was, I was
blindly feeling my way through this move as if I were
a small animal scurrying around a dark basement
with no food in sight—enduring a deprivation from
which I may or may not be able to find my way out.

"Nah," I said. "I don't do it anymore."

He pulled a razor blade out of his pocket, started
separating the powder into groups, then small lines.
"Not even just a bump?" he asked, concentrating on
his desk as if it were a canvas.

This was the first time I'd abstained from everything at once, even sex. I'd been feeling my way
around in my skin without even a hint of anesthesia,
as if standing in a wide-open desert with nothing to
distract myself from thirst; I sensed the potency of
every movement and action, each word spoken and
received. I smelled the coke, its frostbitten essence
hitting me, a perfume of the past painting a picture
of who I once was. *I can do just one,* I thought, but
I didn't let on that I was thinking about it. *How
many years has it been?* With coke, my temptation
depended on the circumstances. With friends who
were recreational, it was harder to pass up, since I
knew I wasn't engaging with people who'd become
angry or irrational if it was taken away—who needed
it, and became ugly without it. I wasn't so sure about
Rick. *Recreational,* I thought. *Functional.*

*

Back before I dated John, when we were friends who
worked together in the restaurant, he used to tell
me, "I walk a fine line." I didn't know, don't think

he knew, that he was warning me—giving me all the signs should I choose to acknowledge them. I didn't know that he was talking about how he'd stay sober from alcohol for weeks, sometimes months, but during these dry periods, he'd use the bathrooms at AA meetings to snort heroin and OxyContin and methadone. I understood the idea of substitution. When I stopped doing hard drugs, I still drank and smoked pot every day, always replacing one thing with the next. But I hoped addiction was somewhat of a choice about how to live—that if you truly wanted to free yourself from it, you could.

Rick leaned his head to the side, the razor blade poised and ready to cut my lines from his.

I answered him. "No, I'm good. Thanks, though."

*

One night, when I lived in Santa Cruz, I sat at a café table outside the bookstore on Pacific Street, trying to muster effective words to put on the page, strong words, with nouns that stood tall and verbs to help me explore a subject outside of myself, but I was having a difficult time.

An older Burmese man approached my table. I'd noticed him drawing a few seats away from where I sat and I'd wondered what he was sketching. He had a small, delicate nose and a smooth complexion. Dark, kind eyes. He introduced himself. "I've been here for five years," he said. "Beautiful place."

I invited him to sit down, and he did. "My country too is beautiful, but very poor. A lot of people suffering." His lips were thick, his face round. He looked up and down the sidewalks at the people, locals and transients, holding signs that said *Impeach Bush* and *Stop the Invasion*. "In our society, people are very caught up with material things, with the drilling of oil, with becoming rich." I nodded, mesmerized by his gentle voice. I listened as if he were a sage who dropped out of the sky with the sole purpose of landing here at my table. "People distract themselves with their big cars and houses. Why not encourage the wealth of the mind, the wealth of the heart? It is crucial to remember what is important in life." He asked where I was from, what I was doing.

"I just needed a change," I said, forcing a smile.

"Santa Cruz is a magical place."

"It is."

When he stood up to leave, he pushed his chair in, and ripped a drawing out of his sketchbook. "This is for you," he said, handing it to me.

I looked at the paper and saw myself. The familiar curve of my chin from the side, eyes wide, hair long and curly and frayed at the bottom. I looked contemplative, serious, my bottom lip pushed up, my mouth squeezed into a pout. Even though it was obviously me, I couldn't help but wonder who this girl was, the expression she wore so foreign, so forlorn.

"I wish you well," he said, as he got up and pushed his chair in. "To peace."

"To peace," I said, and watched him go.

*

Nine years later, on West Cliff Drive, I saw him—not the man from Burma, but John—a visor, the tan cargo pants, his hair the color of desert sand. Gray eyes, light freckles, slight lines around his mouth.

A replica. I saw him across the street from where I was standing, the heat of the sun on my back, the ocean behind me. He was in the driver's seat of a parked jeep, hugging a girl with long black hair, looking past her, as if he spotted me too. The girl's back was toward me, her olive tank top loose, and as he reached around her, I saw the way his hands gripped her waist, grabbling for the certainty of her mid-section's curves, her back's arches. His hands were not large but they were strong, tendons bulging, fingers spread wide, covering the small of her back. His hands: I saw the way they touched my face, my hair—this flash of him and me, of us.

Their goodbye was prolonged—it went on for minutes, as if it wouldn't end, as if they'd change their minds before one of them pulled back and away— as if they'd decide not to part. The willows drooped behind them, their green leaves mingling with the indigo lupine blooming in clusters. A brown pelican flittered from branch to branch, tree to tree. People passed by on bicycles, on scooters; they walked by carrying surfboards above their heads, but neither he nor the girl noticed.

Him going home in the middle of the night when he lived with Hannah. Me going west. Later, him going into rehabs. He had followed me here, nine years later, or I had followed him—I was not sure which, and it didn't matter. What mattered was beyond the flicker of his eyes as he hugged her, this girl standing halfway in between his legs, no intention of letting go any time soon, even though he was obviously off somewhere, the keys in the ignition, taking leave.

*

Rick suggested we have lunch at an Italian restaurant way beyond my budget. "My treat." We sat on the patio, where fake Ficus trees stood in corners; white linen napkins and wine glasses adorned the tables. I wondered if I was underdressed in my baggy halter top under my hooded sweatshirt, linen pants, and my faded, half-broken sandals.

When the waiter approached our table, Rick pointed to the wine list and ordered a bottle of Cabernet. He looked at me. "It's from a vineyard in Santa Rosa. I want you to try it." He sipped his water and opened the menu, his button-down shirt loosened at the collar, exposing a few black chest hairs. "The paninis here are great."

The waiter returned, poured Rick a taste of wine, then filled both of our glasses. I hadn't had a drink since I'd been in Santa Cruz. The smell of the crimson wine was pungent, breathing in our glasses like New England fall waiting to be noticed. I knew it would taste like the smoothness of the air on that first crisp day, slide down my throat with satisfaction. "Can we start with an appetizer of mussels?" he asked, before the waiter walked away.

Rick looked at me over his menu, his mouth tightened, his dimples blending into the seriousness of his face. "Can I ask you a question?"

"Sure." I nodded, taking a big sip of the wine.

"Do you like it?"

"It's delicious." I swallowed it easily. It was too late now to think about what a bad idea this was—the warmth of the wine slunk into my stomach, and spread out from there—tingled my legs, my scalp, my lips. "Is that your question?"

"Good, I'm glad you like it. No, I was wondering… what is it that you do at your desk all day? What's that big binder you carry around? Are you studying?"

"No, it's writing. I write," My voice, to my own ears, sounded like a five-year-old's. I'd wanted to be a writer since I was a kid, but I had considered it impossible. Mostly, words served as a way to express the way my father hated me; in my journals, I'd compare him to God and speculate about which degree of abomination was worse. Or, I had written when I was high, fabricated characters who wanted to break out of their hometowns, who felt misunderstood, who sought ways to sever the boundaries that had been created for them by their own fathers or wives or Gods.

Now, I had piles upon piles of half-finished stories and poems and essays, but I had no idea how to shape them into anything readable.

"You know, poems and stories—it's nothing."

"That's cool. It's great. It isn't nothing." Rick tilted his head, dragged his forefinger around the smooth rim of his wine glass. "I just want to know more about you, that's all."

I knew what Rick was thinking. I didn't feel a mutual need to know him, but it was nice to have some company—to get out of my head for a couple of hours.

We ordered another bottle of wine, and by the time we left the restaurant, we were drunk, or at least I was. "Should we go ride the rollercoaster?" Rick asked, his hands in the pockets of his khakis as he turned his head in the direction of the famous boardwalk, where the 1980s movie *The Lost Boys* was filmed.

"Don't we have to go back to work?" I asked.

His eyes darted up, then down my body. "Nah, let me show you some fun."

*

Nine years later, on the Sunday of my four-day visit to Santa Cruz, I went to Dance Church. The back doors were open, the hard wood floor waxed. Candles and incense burned on the altar, crowded by medallions and saints and icons. The music was slow at first, instrumental—the piano, a violin, a pipe organ. We began on the floor, sitting cross legged or lying in fetal positions or corpse pose. People slowly contorted their bodies into bridges, or stood on their heads, legs arched toward the walls. I stood up, my bare feet against the cold floor.

When the first song rolled into the next, the music sped up, and African drums pulsated in my ears. Then flutes and harps and lyres. Wafts of Nag champa lingered, its sweetness meshed with scents of sweat, of earth and soil. I found a familiar calm here. A calm that helped to alleviate the tension in my hips, in between my shoulder blades, in the glands on the sides of my neck, up into my ears, the crown of my head. I danced alone, as I always did. I noticed the way others kicked their feet, leaned into and pushed off one another's bodies. The people in the room had established collaborated rhythms, had transferred heat to and from one another week after week. They lifted and dipped one another, clasped hands in mid movement; they gestured like mimes, splayed aerial silk that streamed across the room.

When I lived here, this was the one place where I

acknowledged the fact that I was a carnal being—experienced the closeness of flesh and skin and bodies that was otherwise absent from my life. I looked forward to Sundays. I looked forward to blending into the herds of people, sharing a space, meeting a set of eyes, grazing a hand. Each week, I stayed the entire way through. For the full two and a half hours I curved my waist, shook and flailed, jumped up and crouched down, waved my arms, whirled around. I tried to channel my grandfather. As I became lost in my own movement, my heated limbs loose, the music became part of me, and I imagined his spirit sweeping down, lifting my body until it became lighter, freer. Back then, I grew sad when the session came to a close, when we stilled ourselves and joined hands while the leader talked for a minute or two, usually offering a tidbit about self-evolution, or a philosophy about the state of the country, the impending war, and always a bit about gratitude. We prayed for change.

But upon my return, as I watched people press their backs and chests against one another's, glistening skin slide to and fro, I realized that I was the only one dancing alone. I moved with a consciousness I didn't remember having before. Nine years before, I had such fresh pain, raw pain, that it overrode any inhibitions. *This time*, I thought, *I want to leave all my pain here in this city.* But I was no longer the person I was when I'd taken off to California that summer. I had known this, but it was magnified in this room where I watched the girl I used to be, who danced always near the door, this girl who took exit signs seriously, this girl unsure of how to hold on to any type of love, and who, once finding it, gave it away without thought, left herself with nothing.

This return trip was four days long, and while I could have stretched it out longer, I didn't feel the need to. The distress I once felt in this town, the feeling of being broken to bits—it wasn't mine any longer. Time had released me; the pain had been lost.

But then, when I least expected it, it crept up in a dream.

*

It begins in the dark basement of a restaurant. I don't recognize the place, but in the dream it seems normal that we're all sitting there on silver folding chairs in a circle in the dark. We've probably just passed a joint out of sight of cameras or windows, the way people in restaurants do when it's time to decompress after long, busy nights.

"Come with us," you say, and I look up at the sound of your voice. I see that it is you, the familiar outline of your silhouette, the red glow of your cigarette like an ember illuminating our past. At first, I'm surprised to see you after all this time—it is both unreal and expected, like déjà vu. You smile at me as if not a day has passed, and I recognize the fullness, the shape of your lips, the way you hold your cigarette way down between your index and middle fingers, close to the crease between them. I hear the way you draw out my name, the way you accentuate the invitation. *"Come with us."*

I look around the circle, see who else is there, and recognize one of the younger guys as someone we have worked with. He's looking back and forth between us—he has known us together, and he knows the decision I will make. That for me you have been a diversion from the things about myself I never wanted to face: the way I let my father rip through me, the fear of my volatile reactions to his words, his anger, the way I want to forgive him but cannot. The way I have never wanted, will never have a child, but felt a nagging love for yours, one I could not shed after you both were gone.

Before I know what I'm doing, we're getting into a car with a few other people, you and I crammed in the backseat, pressed against one another, your hand on my leg, and you are saying, "I am going to get clean this time." You speak of a dream I don't remember having. You fix your eyes on mine, the way you always did—your mouth holding me, as if to say, *I mean it this time.* I'm faced with a daunting decision; I know I want to stay in the car with you, ride to anywhere, but I also know I'll be risking everything. *What am I doing?* We drive on in darkness in the rain, and before I have a chance to answer myself, cops surround us—the blue lights blinding, the sirens deafening. There are four police cars, one on each side, one at each end of the car. *Shit.* The speakers blare: "Step out of the vehicle." The ride stops here, and I wake up.

When I woke up from this three-dimensional dream in a strange bed, I was on a writing retreat hundreds of miles from home. When I woke up, my sadness was so potent that I still felt my body slither across the car's seat, the bitter leather scent mixed with smoke, still tasted the mint on your breath. It was as if I hadn't woken at all. I waded through the weight of this dream as if trudging through flooded streets, the sorrow stinging me like winter rain. I told a stranger about it—about its visceral nature, about the way I sensed its metaphorical truth in the core of my body as if having been cut open during the night.

I wanted to remember you exactly as you were in the one picture I still had—cheeks and chin scruff with the beginnings of a beard, your eyes those of having lived, your face content with the comfort of Jacob's arm around your neck, his fingertips on your skin, your heads pressed together. Jacob, the prophet who came to save you.

*

I decided I would sleep with him—my boss, Rick—just once. I wanted to remember what it was like to feel a man's body on top of, underneath, beside, inside of mine. It had been too long. I was going to leave Santa Cruz, go back to New Hampshire for a month to save some money, and then head to the Virgin Islands for the winter, so I figured any regrets would stay here behind me, in the west.

My co-workers wanted to throw me a party, so I invited them to my house. I drank vodka with club soda and lemons after three months of sobriety, minus the drunken lunch outing with Rick. Since I no longer had a tolerance for alcohol, the night of the party became a blur. Photos confirmed what my memory did not—that we were out on the back deck laughing, smoking cigarettes and joints, the boombox probably playing Fleetwood Mac, or The Dead. I do recall my work friends lining up in the hallway outside the bath-room door, entering in groups, obviously doing lines, but I was drunk enough to ignore it. I also remember sitting next to Rick on the couch, my legs scrunched up so my knees were on top of his thighs—we may or may not have kissed. Not long after, I threw up in the bathroom, the toilet bowl spinning, and I went to bed without saying goodbye to anyone.

The next day, I'd already forgotten about the longing for sex, about the people I'd met and worked with in this city. My head pounded as I sat at the kitchen table and pulled out my atlas. I flipped through the pages and mapped out my route, shaded in the states that would lead me home.

*

The day I left Santa Cruz after my four-day return, I drove across the San Francisco bridges, then south on Highway 1 to Half Moon Bay. People were camped in sandy spots along the road, parked in RVs shaded by cottonwoods. Herring gulls inched along the sand, their mouths clenching starfish. Waves crashed onto the rocky ledges and formed crystals as the sun broke through the sky. I was overwhelmed by beauty, caught in a state of transience, transition. Moving to get somewhere from here.

That morning, on West Cliff Drive, I sat on a bench built in the memory of two people with the same last name, and I thought about timeless moments, the ones that remain even as we outgrow them, the snapshots we carry with us. Our lovers' scents, our grandfathers' hands. These details shift and shape themselves again and again, flash with different degrees of prominence, push and bury others into the background. I gripped the bench, its rounded corners, its spots worn from the blasting of the sun and wind, the salt of the bay, the weight of the passersby; I imagined how it had been altered since it was first made. Its details, like ours, have been created, modified by the elements, grooved and cracked, touched up and polished, tarnished and perfected by our memories, the way we have chosen to assemble and compile them, engrave them into our minds. The structure of the wood, the flaws that have become part of it now part of a much larger landscape.

On the way back east, during the lift into the sky, I looked out the window as the plane pushed upward, the images of land and water zooming out, buildings and roads becoming miniature strokes from a paintbrush, a house the size of a hand, smaller and smaller, then gone. We ascended into the clouds stretched across the sky like gauze, luminous streams of pink and yellow and orange streaking the atmosphere. Gravity surrendered as I pulled away from the world beneath me—the redwoods, the mountains, the ocean, the girl sitting on the bench all melting away. The entire picture full of heartbreak, full of hope.

*

So much of this narrative is about the inability to be alone, to live with oneself. It was Kafka who wrote often about the solitude necessary for a writer. And it is true that writing requires a person to be alone with oneself for hours on end, to obtain respite from the noise of one's surroundings, which for a long while, was impossible for me to do.

After John had left for good, I saw a flier for writing classes held inside the home of a local woman. She offered the classes for eight weeks at a time, and I signed up for session after session, treating these groups like a religious practice. I attended days and evenings, participated in as many as I could afford. But it would still take years for me to inhabit the type of solitude necessary to delve deep inside myself, a solitude that I feared intensely, my restless self in a constant state of indecision, thrashing around in movement while wearing an invisible, weighted blanket that always kept me in the exact same place. I saw a therapist, attempted meditation, became focused on the health of my body. But it was the discipline and practice of writing, the habitual nature of concentration, that helped to alleviate the darkness of my world, that finally allowed me to be content in stillness.

As I sit at a homemade desk in a coastal Maine town where I live with Derek, my boyfriend of more than a decade, I put pencil to paper for hours upon hours. I spend entire days in this small room surrounded by books, eloquent poems and quotes by my favorite authors hanging on the walls. While I work, I am reminded that the fear that is still—from time to time, able to grip me like a starving predator—is only an illusion, a state of mind and perception—that escape exists.

I work in the summertime, the breeze blowing in through the window's screen, the sound of the lawnmower's engine humming outside, of wood being cut and stacked, the smell of a neighbor's grill. After a while, the front door opens, and Derek pokes his head in to ask how it's going. "Ready for a break?"

I make a few last notes and save my work, follow him outside, take a deep breath of the breezeless, humid air. He waits in the driveway while I put my helmet over my head, and climb onto the back of his motorcycle. It's close to evening, and the New England sun burns brightly in the sky after so many months of dead, cold winter—of broken, gray skies.

We take off down the road, the noise of the bike in my ears, and we weave along the pavement, meander up and down hills. I have one hand on the seat's strap, and my inner thighs hold Derek's hips, my hair fluttering around my eyes. We travel the back roads of surrounding towns, the streets lined with blue spruce pines. Trails of green blaze by us.

The wind whips across my chest and shoulders and arms, and the vibrations of the bike rip through me, relaxing the muscle fibers of my neck and back, softening my limbs. We fly by the pond patched with lily pads, the lawns bursting with purple hydrangeas, the marshy smell of salt, of summer. People stand on bridges, their fishing lines cast into the river. The water is lined with boats and paddleboards, the sky a blast of blue streaming with white and a hint of purple. The warm air heats my skin, and I find myself fully inside these moments, but as if I am lifted from my body at the same time, a sensation I can only compare with the surreal experience I encounter when making art.

I think of how, as I generate a piece of writing, I have flickering realizations that I am no more the creator of the work than part of the process of creating it— language and syntax scribed, released into the atmosphere, recycling into a world I re-envision time and time again, like the worlds recreated in this story. How these moments actually take me out of myself and into something greater, every sweet smell of lilac, every drink of outside air, each silvery raindrop glistening on a naked tree branch bringing me back to this solo endeavor that grants me relief, prompts me to walk outside and plant my feet on the dirt and dandelions, to find myself at home.

ACKNOWLEDGMENTS

I am beyond grateful for the multitude of people who have contributed to the crafting of this book. Thank you to the editors of the following journals, in which chapters or pieces of this work originally appeared: *Under the Sun, Gettysburg Review, Fourth Genre, Flyway: Journal of Writing & Environment, The Clackamas Literary Review, Silk Road Review, Fugue, The Concho River Review, Sycamore Review, PMSpoemmemoirstory, Best New Writing 2010,* and *Hope Whispers*. Thank you to the judges of the following contests, who recognized this manuscript as a finalist: the 2020 Robert C. Jones Prize for Short Prose, the 2018 Autumn House Press Full-Length Contest, the 2015 Zone 3 Press Creative Nonfiction Book Award, the 2013 William Faulkner-William Wisdom Narrative Nonfiction Prize, the 2012 Autumn House Press Nonfiction Prize, and the 2012 SouthWest Writers Competition.

I am indebted to the wonderful people at Vine Leaves Press, especially Jessica Bell and Amie McCracken, for believing in this book, and Melanie Faith, my inspiring and talented editor, for her attention to detail, her enthusiasm, and for encouraging me to probe deeper.

I have an overwhelming amount of gratitude for the beautiful writers in my life, many of whom have read draft upon draft of this work in so many incarnations, over a period of years, and all of whom have offered meaningful conversations, precise visions, and solid, grounding advice: Anthony D'Aries, Adrienne Jaeger, Christy Woods, Meghan Cadwallader, Susan Casey, Michelle Metcalf, Michelle Cacho-Negrete, Kayenta Williams, Beth Slattery, Lesley Heiser, Nancy Brown, Gro Flatebo, Barbara Walsh, Rita Saliba, Amy Carpenter, Kerry Herlihy, Morgan Callan Rogers, Jean Peck, Andrea Vasquez, Hilary McQuilkin, Lisa Wilson, and Will Conway.

Thank you to my exceptional Stonecoast MFA mentors: Baron Wormser, Joan Connor, Debra Marquart, and Barbara Hurd. My admiration and appreciation for you is infinite. Without you, this would never be a book.

Thank you to the following readers, all brilliant writers, for your time and generosity: Sue William Silverman, Tim Hillegonds, Fleda Brown, Domenica Ruta, Suzanne Strempek Shea, Martha Highers, Angela Palm, Lidia Yuknavitch, Sonya Huber, and Meredith Hall. Thank you to the folks at Randolph College, particularly Bunny Goodjohn, for your warm welcome, for being an exceptional host, and for the space and time to create.

To the Ireland Dinglings, for your friendship and laughter, and your keen editorial eyes: Carol Berg, Taryn Bowe, Dawn LeMay, Christine Tierney, Erin Underwood, Alison McMahan, Suzanne Van Dam, Arla Ralston, Annie Deppe, and Ted Deppe.

I'd like to thank Susan Mohaghegh, who granted me with a creative outlet at a time when I needed it most. Big love to MK, for your wise, deliberate assur-